In Dubious Terrain

Lyric and Conjecture

In Dubious Terrain

Lyric and Conjecture

by

DB Jonas

© 2026 DB Jonas. All rights reserved.
This material may not be reproduced in any form, published,
reprinted, recorded, performed, broadcast,
rewritten or redistributed without
the explicit permission of DB Jonas.
All such actions are strictly prohibited by law.

Cover design by Shay Culligan
Cover image by Grant Faint, courtesy of Getty Images

ISBN: 979-8-90146-712-1
Library of Congress Control Number: 202693447

Kelsay Books
502 South 1040 East, A-119
American Fork, Utah 84003
Kelsaybooks.com

Dedicated to the lingering voices
of Emmanuel Levinas and Maurice Blanchot,
the necessary angels of our understanding,
and of Joe Libertson, incomparable reader,
thinker, and indispensable guide,

and to Julie, as ever,
who makes all the inscrutable meanings
meaningful.

Acknowledgments

The following poems and prose-pieces first appeared in these journals:

The Amphibian: "The Misery Machine"
Black Works: "The Dreaming Dreams the Dreamer"
Blue Unicorn: "Fabric of this Air"
Cathexis Northwest Press: "Art Appreciation"
The Deronda Review: "Before Deciding," "Following the Law"
The Ekphrastic Review: "Ut pictura poesis" (as "Lebens ohne Eigenschaften")
The Eunoia Review: "Wool-Gathering," "In Sympathy"
The Galway Review: "Urgent Message to K2-18b," "Their Fierce Phonetics," "Closer," "Animations," "She Who Speaks," "Ubi sunt?"
Jerry Jazz Musician: "Radio Nights," "Under the Influence"
Journal of Humanistic Mathematics: "Yet No Ramanujan," "Archimedes Dreaming"
The Orchards Poetry Journal: "Between the Saying and the Said," "The Visitor"
Poets for Science: "Fibonacci at the Tide-Pools"
The Purpled Nail: "Post Mortem"
The Ravens Perch: "Dawn Balloon at Anza-Borrego," "Bioenergetics," "Land of Unlikelihood / Land of Unlikeness," "The Unnameable"
Trouvaille Review: "Older Than Things"
Unbroken Journal: "In Solitary," "God Walks into a Bar," "In the Beginning"

Contents

II. The Noise of Numbers

III. Of Interiors

I.
Patience of the Words

I know only one
thing to talk
about (poetry)
and that
covers everything.
—A.R. Ammons, *One Loves*

No Art

No art can furnish
evidence of you.
You're not remotely

what it's all about.
No one can draw
a line from it to you,

from there to here,
from what must,
rising into flesh,

emerge concrete,
vascular, incarnate
in the tooling hand,

the spooling brain,
appear as if by fiat
from the air, from

something never
there before, yet
somehow cork-

screws oddly
upward into life,
arisen with its

own peculiar odor
from the compost
of your own precise

disorder. And just
like you, your art's
no product,

much less sum,
of anything you are
or might become,

but something made
from what remains
undone, abandoned,

misremembered, left
unread, unpictured,
left unsaid.

The Instruction

Kafka to Brod

Each song that's made of air, that gathers only shadow,
only weightless time around it, lingers barely long
enough to hear its insubstantial music softly fade,
its labored breath retreating from comparison,
from judgment and appreciation, from all the voices
that contest to fill the room with ample evidence
of their triumphant presence here, of this relentless chase,
this journeying, its desultory defeats and dominations.

The damned, though, beloved of gods, seem to some-
how be aware their time is short yet infinitely slow,
and in the end require that every sheet be set afire,
each scrap of thought consigned to ash, to the dust
from which it rose to mar their perfect silences,
that every utterance unsettle comprehension
and every story hurry toward conclusion, where every
road converge to ascertain that each song's shorn
of all except the ultimate in things, all beside obsession,
all else beside the thrumming of incessant repetition.

One Way or Another

As ever, as always,
it's always on the way,
or barely just departed.

It makes a sound
like dawn does,
like daybreak, like
the sound trains make
on their cautious way
into the station.

So painfully slow,
its only time-frame
is its endless *rallentando,*
its arrival in a time
without direction,
the time of what's
not ever yet, or what
has been and long
since gone, of something
left behind, the empty wake
of misconnection,
the lonesome whistle
and seismic rumble
of what's not there.

Like the dawn,
its arrival coincides
with its departure.
Like dawn, it is only
what's in transit:
something near
but never to appear,
irretrievable and unavoidable,
and always on the verge
of a return.

Beyond Measure

to a cover photo on a book of poems

This morning's room
has only room enough
for the two of us,
for the empty street,
for the desolate gusts
from off the docks
that sweep the grime-
caked sidewalks clean,
for the unwarm sun
that slices through
the elevated tracks,
for the faint departing sound
of someone else's train,
for all of this and me.

For all there really is,
it seems, is just
the two of us:
myself and what is
not myself, myself
and what's not there,
but will not go away,
this place without
a decent place to hide,
where I'm the stranger,
and the stranger there
is me, this silhouette,
this opacity, this one
with whom I'll never
coincide.

Rallentando

of verbality and velocity

The temporizing word drags its feet. It scuffles over the Empty Quarters of consciousness. The sound it leaves behind or broadcasts in advance of its denotations, its excess over meaning, is like the slowing noise that trains make on their approach to the terminal. Like light, the sonority of words, irreducible to what's signified, approaching from a point of departure seemingly beyond all calculable distance, may be imagined to radiate outward in time (assuming the role of time itself, you might say), in a time seemingly without end, its spectral wavelength off the map, far too weak to die. If the speed of light is the limit velocity of the universe, could it be that the halting motility of speech, the domain of the spoken, of words once heard, overheard, mis-heard, read, misread, signed, recollected, misremembered, imagined, dreamed, can be said to approach the glacial limits of languor, the minimal inertial tempo of that which is not, theoretically at least, absolutely inert, not, kinematically speaking, quite at rest?

Our sentient life begins in vibration, in the pitch-dark auscultations of an amniotic life. Yet language is an aspect of our native velocity as bodies in motion. We are swept up by words as we are swept up in time, always hurtled forward, if imperceptibly, into the indeterminate. We cannot feel their breeze against our skin. At every moment, we are driven forward and distracted by desire, impelled by the urgency of self-assertion. Early on, in infancy, we learn to employ our voices in pursuit of our desires, to insert ourselves into the noisy rush and to establish a presence, an identity, shouldering our way into the common ruckus of vocal expression, the noisy world of signs, its violence, the raucous stream of speech.

In light of this paradox, the song, the poem, the performative word's appropriation of language, can seem to operate altogether differently than the media of self-assertion in which we live. There is something subversive in it, disorienting. Its alarming indirection, its tendency to digression and distraction, hijacked by thrumming intonation from pathways of intentional "expression," can slow us to a crawl, stop us in our tracks, decelerate our breathless progress through the world and lift us, like music, as music does, out of the stream of things, away from the breathless logic of utility. This hebetude, this inhuman slowness, is something that the maker of song might just discover as a reader, long before she's rediscovered it as a writer. A soliloquy of Shakespeare, an ode of Keats, the stillness of some lines from Bashō or Char, Hardy or Dickinson, can arrest, if only for a fleeting moment, the breathless hellbent declamations of linear thought. Their intrusions and interruptions can place us in a strange hiatus, in alien terrain, as if suspended in time. Their *cognitive music,* as a critic once put it, may give us pause.

This slowness in song, the slowness of lyric thought, is fundamental to its peculiar character in the world of words, it seems to me, a curious phenomenality essential to the experience of reading, of listening to, and of making song. Like all works of what we call art, the dislocations they induce seem to arise from the irreducibly alien atmospheres they gather around them. Cloaked in the familiar language of the everyday, these aberrant acts of speech efface their biographical speaker and disorient their hearers, slowing life to a crawl. This obstinate *ritardando* in poetry, this *rallentando* or freakish *allargando* of the words, these oddities of speech, may account for their lingering quality, perhaps, and for the indirection fundamental to their expressivity, their awkwardness, their radical impersonality, their tendency to loiter aimlessly, to stimulate our thought and to eternally return, to always unexpectedly repeat, in the reader's grimly determined, self-asserting, denotating, forward-focused, purposeful mind.

His Heuristic

All his poems seem
to leave behind
the swirling sound
of educated guesses,

an itch or stitch
of indeterminate
location, an abscess
at the flawless surface

of your thought,
some excess baggage
you do not recognize
as yours, suspended,

weightless, audible
only in the undetected
tick of what's escaped
your observation,

unrecognized,
unnamed, an infinitely
patient thing beneath
the hood that loiters

in the near vicinity
of denotation,
an improvised device,
loaded, primed, implanted

in the transient logic
of your idling dream,
deathless, and patiently
awaiting detonation.

Art Appreciation

Strictly speaking, he was only an impediment
on the way to the menagerie.
—Franz Kafka, *Ein Hungerkünstler*

The noise that drifted
up to us in the otherwise
empty gallery
was nothing human,
something rather like
what we'd expect
from a loosened drainpipe
or desiccated seedpod
rattling in the wind,
a rusty hinge, a groan
of faulty plumbing
in the wall.

Before too long,
we connoisseurs of tedium
had wearied of this slow
uneasy art of his,
an art composed
of quietude, the art
of simply sitting there
and doing nothing,
a masterpiece of grim
refusal, demanding only
that he softly disappear
into the pile of dirty rags
where he'd at first
presumed to be

. . . and bit by bit,
to not be any

longer there at all,
being nothing but
the empty spectacle
of an art that's left
behind itself
a space where there
was nothing left of him
beside the endless ache
of his peculiar vacancy,
this hollowed evidence,
this void he'd left suspended
in the air. And, one by one,
we just stopped coming.

But he continued on
upon that little platform,
nonetheless, that pile
of straw out there
for anyone who cared
to see, and those vanishing
few who did can't help
but ever after sense
the viscous presence
of his absentness,
can't manage to suppress
the unfamiliar sound,
the noiseless groan,
of that benign, anonymous,
unquiet emptiness.

Letter to Paul Antschel

poste restante

How is it that such weariness persists
to outlast strength, to fetch such
heavy buckets from the well of years,
to undertake those endless journeys
and release such countless soundings
into the dizzying well of words?

How close at hand
must all such wellsprings be
to meet the splash of sounding stone,
to meet the falling sound
of fallen song, to answer
all those voices burning
through the hostile night,
to devastate, confound, delight
and gather you!

Gregor Samsa

What is it but the words again
have pinned me to the spot I'm in,
this thorax wobbly as a mandolin,
the waving tangle of these disarticulated
limbs, this ceaseless hirsute clawing at the air,
my nauseating happenstance at last
made manifest down here beneath the distant
ceiling of my room, a morning's room
awash in last night's kitchen smells
and every feral pheromone, the scent of glue
from underneath the faded wallpaper, and how
that odd mandibular clacking sound I make's
my one remaining gesture of desperation,
my one remaining chance at what might pass
for genial conversation?

Is this some transient phase, or what
I've always been? Surely it's this writing
habit that has fashioned the revolting creature
I've become. And the horror in those faces
peering from the door, the swift slam shut,
might indicate that this most inconvenient sheath
I've woven's nothing more than daylight's
wiggling nymph, a morning's instar, trick
of light, a brittle, translucent, transitory thing,
but then again, they'd frequently looked in at me
like this at dawn in their bewilderment,
in their alarm, this gaping unfamiliar family
of mine that huddles in my efflorescent insect brain
beneath the steady ticking of the tallcase clock,

basking in the warm embrace of all life's
comforting conventions, the stern authority
of hard-earned *Heimlichkeit,* their righteous
trepidations and their shame.

These furtive scratching sounds I make,
the tracery that all this scrabbling diffidence
can't manage but to leave behind, are all
that's left for me to offer, since I'm nothing
other than the thing I do or must have done,
a thing without clear purpose, a creature
shipwrecked on these rumpled sheets,
homeless in the warm embrace of home,
out of place and always out of season,
the appalling, crawling consequence
of this hapless skittering pen, this boundless,
senseless, scrawling reason.

The Absence of an Ending

How shall we make an end of stories
made from air, our tales devoid
of dire protagonists, devoid of struggle,
plot, or obstacle, innocent of any telling
detail, skulking menace, looming threat?

How do we bring to its conclusion
each inconclusive, diffident account
of just what happens, just what's there,
of what occurs without apparent
cause or edifying consequence?

Your readers hold their patient breath
in hopes some other shoe might drop,
but in consideration of the wiggling thing
you've planted in that reader's brain,
what's left to do but stop?

Our Troublesome Opacities

This means stepping out of what's human.
—P. Celan, *The Meridian*

Yes, there must be, so that words
might stand erect and might appear,
some adamantine rectitude, some
obstinate opacity, an armature of iron,
an exoskeleton of steel, a solemnity
that defies the reader's quaint fixations,
resists her eager, deadly, basilisk gaze.

There must be some moment where
it all goes haywire in the reader's
mind, where vagrant words annihilate
as well the speaker's share, turn heel
on all intention, rebuff your knowing
comprehension, and evict the reader
and the writer both from quietude,
the cozy room, the glib detachment
of their isolated observation place
somewhere there outside the poem.

Yet this opacity's no strength in art.
It's not a potency that artworks have,
but the weakness at their rootless heart,
their inability to tell you just exactly
what they mean, the way they'll turn

away from meaning into the wind,
lips moving, inarticulate, what Celan
calls their Breathturn, their *Atemwende,*
and seem to pivot toward what's always
Other, other than the one specific other
that the sympathetic reader, each astute
beholder, seeks to be.

The impenetrable's that serious bit
that always lingers on, the extra puzzle-
piece that won't quite fit, that irksome
residue that sits outside the framework
of intention, resists our sparkling
intellect, and cannot be explained away:
that element in art that brazenly defies us
as it yields, escapes as it surrenders,
and generates new meaning as it runs
like fascination, ripples out like mirth,
like spillage, like an irksome excess
in our speaking, a remainder unresolved,
unresolvable, unavoidable, inhuman,
where words and images might intimate,
mean always otherwise, mean infinitely
more, than they can ever possibly mean.

Churlish Apologia

This is, when all is said and done,
an earnest effort to make sense,
make both sense and sensibility
of just what's there along with what
is not, allow this world of thought,
the world we're held within,
to think again and somehow feel,
to understand itself as consequence,
the consequence of happenstance,
while hoping not, while we are at it,
to loose this louche devouring intellect
upon the twistings of complexity, reduce
this amplitude that is our life to what
can be contained or what purports
to be the sum of all there is, to that
which seeks to speak in simple terms
some simple Truth, but try instead
to hear what whispers in the wounded
words, to comprehend this gravity
that's larger than their meanings,
to intimate what is not ever there
to speak, yet never ceases speaking.

Solitary Sonneteer

Your words are like a clothesline strung
between the thought you had and some
imagined someone else's distant flesh,
a filament, a fragile length of leader,
a slender wire fastened onto someplace
we'll call A and somewhere else out there,
some B the darkness doesn't let you see.

And you, the cautious inching aerialist
who feels his way along that thought,
that narrow road made only of extension,
the path it takes you down, its slim direction
devoid of all dimension but the hopeless hope
that somewhere past the limit of your rope
those words might find some destination.

Between the Saying and the Said

What might saying mean
before it signifies what's said?
—E. Levinas, *Le Dit et le Dire*

Try then once again, as try you might,
to find the speaking in the spoken,
and in these transient words that write,
transfix the writing in the written.

You try to be, with all your might,
the one who speaks and understands,
the one who silences the moving pen
and stills the moving hand.

You see yourself aloft, alone, adrift
atop the whirling midst of things,
alert upon the stable center of your dream,
stark witness to what was or is or seems,

but unexpected words return to you
before they can arrive
to signify what's not yet here
and give what isn't yours to give.

Their faint archaic voices speak
between the saying and the said,
those rumors from the life you've led,
those rumblings from the dead.

Of Meaning and Beauty

And yet it was never beauty we were after. Not the melodious effects of beautified language, but the beauty always there in language, the beauty that is language, a soft pulsation, the shallow breathing of a fragile thing that manages to survive our anxious custody, to make its perilous passage home from the field and back out into song. Beauty, if beauty there be, has somehow had to find a path to song for us, attach itself haphazardly to the curious enterprise of song, to its endless scuffling and journeying, and so assume the role of aviary or a botanizer's Wardian Case, a mason jar of pond-water, a perch-stand, framework or membrane where the singing might be gathered, set apart, be found to harbor meaning, contain a thing far larger than itself, convey some vital sliver of the real.

Regard the beauty in our languages, the unadorned sonorities of speaking, not cherry-picked to fit our purpose, but the relentless engendering of what in all our speaking bears the seed of its undoing as a useful medium or bridge connecting the sender to some receiver, as the ping-ponging, back-and-forthing symmetry of our endless coding and decoding, our life among others.

The painfully lengthy, languorous task of hapless song, its hopeless if unconscious object, can seem sometimes to undermine the stout foundations of our gift of speech, to quietly undo the idiom it deploys, to modestly disrupt all grammars and conventions, the logics we assume as givens, with the pulsing energy of the purposeless, the ineffectual, of what has no business being there, and to thus undo all our earnest intentions, our desperate need to communicate, to convey some proof of our existence in the distracting, disorienting, carnal and unaccountable presence of beauty.

What remains are the oscillations of voice, its lingering intonations, an energy liberated from the tyranny of craft and personality, prosody and rhetoric, simile and metaphor, something animal, anonymous, unfamiliar, unmistakable, unconcerned with denotations and connotations, destitute of sign and symbol, of sincerity and irony, truth and falsehood, a savage beauty haplessly enmeshed in language, hopelessly inextricable from meaning.

Fabric of this Air

of George Herbert and the serious in poetry

The paradox that grips your thought
is no conniving artifice of speech, is not
the telltale rattle of the trickster's quiver, not
so much the fabrication of your nimble mind,
as the evidence in which mind is caught.

These metaphors that wander in the words,
not devilish devisings, no stratagems of yours,
compose the soil upon which thought occurs,
comprise the breathing substance of all out there
that you address, to which all reasoning refers.

Try then mightily to say one thing in isolation,
as lawyers do, no firm intention left undone,
but words unweave their many from your one,
and world its multitude from dogged denotation.

Wool-Gathering

The writing is this listening, to write is to listen.
I don't plan anything. Writing happens.
—Jon Fosse

You take your inspiration from the weaving air itself,
your rhythms woven from the braided noise of life,
the nervous twitch of time, the soft-sprung metrics
of the speaking world, the gauzy prosody that swirls
in quiet rooms, the warp and weft of breath, those things
you cannot somehow fail to hear, the way the words
appear to climb and wrap themselves around them-
selves as sound convolves with sound, arisen out
of nowhere, from the helical surfaces of speech
where meanings knit their fibrous filaments and turn
and turn, where all there is is texture, all is mote-filled light,
where all is just the density that gathers as vibration,
where yours is not to fabricate or make things clear,
to knit or braid or twist, but just to listen and to hear.

The Flesh of Song

But whose song is it? Who is it, really, *what* is it, that sings? We like to say we may identify a poet by her voice, by the features of that one precise, inimitable intonation, the unmistakable noise her thinking makes. *Give me two bars, and I'll tell you whether it's Richter or Rubinstein, Jandó, Serkin or Arrau,* we'll say. And we're not wrong to identify the peculiar voice in some distinctive keyboardist's attack or the wild inhuman clamor released into the world by this or that singular breath or embouchure, the angled pressure of a bow, the resonance that issues from the length and tautness of those peculiar vocal folds or by the microscopic shares of flesh and nail involved in all the plucks and scrapes and *rasqueados,* the stops, the tremors, the *rubati* and *glissandi* that concentrate upon the strings to offer some coherent, resonating thought produced in some specific resonant body by some distinctly resonant mind.

And composition cannot ever free itself entirely from performance, since it is always already a phenomenon rooted in performance, however unshared in practice, rooted in the haptic universe of contact and interiority, the carnal world of sonority and shimmering image, mimicry, abstraction and urgent if inscrutable meaning. Henri Michaux speaks of the sanzas, *an instrument that can hardly be heard; it is played in Africa for oneself alone, . . . rudimentary, archaic, apparently put together haphazardly, freely, by the village blacksmith . . . no two of them the same . . . independent of any scale. Anarchical. A music of murmurs.*[1]

[1] Translation by David Ball, *Face à qui se dérobe* in *Darkness Moves*

Such perhaps is the voice we say we hear in song. Peculiar, unique, but in the end impersonal in its intimacy, its artless solipsism, arising from the abstract, independent of any score, *independent of any scale.* It arises, perhaps, not as coded messages arise, from the gap between ourselves and the maker of songs, the empty interval that separates a performer from her audience, from the shared mediations of a common language or tonal system, but in the unmediated carnality of our nervous systems, the primacy of our exposure to the world, to vibration, to meanings irreducible to messages: a cognitive noise, immediate, seductive, alien and inescapable. It is the inescapable voice, the alien sensibilities, the jarring syntax, tonal and rhythmic patterns, and unexpected word-choices of the stranger, the irreducibly other.

So what is it, in the end, that sings? Perhaps it's what, in the singular soundscape of the remote and peculiar, and only there, in what lies impossibly distant yet somehow also disturbingly close, sings to us of what we already know, of where we've always been, of what we ourselves improbably are.

Older Than Things

The world of sound immersed us early on,
before the world of things appeared, when
light and shadow chortled in our hazy sight
amid the chortling throb of mother-words
that galvanized our skin.

The buzzing noise of houseflies in the room,
the distant ring of voices in the hall, the silences
that whispered in the anxious dark,
the tidal weightlessness that dandled, swayed
and cooled our plummy infant flesh

persists throughout the noisy place we wander in
to vex the busy day and interrupt the night,
to animate the raucous stream of speech
that rises from our throats, the grasping words
we each routinely use to capture what we want.

No wonder then that poetry just can't remain
within the bounds of our intention, but wanders
hapless through that subaquatic realm of sound,
that time before the visible, a universe more ancient
than the self, much older than the world of things.

Their Fierce Phonetics

At the edge of the alphabet there is no safeguard against the dead.
—Janet Frame, *The Edge of the Alphabet*

All the sounds, to them, took place as shapes,
the sounds that formed in the mouths of others,
in the silenced speech of written words, the noisy
street, the gurgling ditch, the whir and murmur
of a million fans and motors, daylight's ceaseless
drone, the peeps and squeaks that interrupt
each bosomy, cradling night.

But it was spoken words, their specific gravities,
light as pumice, heavy as basalt, the way they
cleared a place and filled it in the mouth, the shape
they made along the haptic tongue, their anxious
rasp against the teeth, their surface planes, their
edges cool, abrasive, jagged, ridged, their awkward
weights and densities, the gutturals that gathered
in the air and clustered in the throat.

So it had been so easy for them, for us, to locate
words once heard, impossible to mislay the shapes
that filled the ear, the eye, the cradling palate,
once their curious weight had settled in, once
they had arrived like gifts, occurred like losses,
left to bloom like crystals in the dripping dark.

And their elegant mouth-feel, each textured surface
tumbled, chafed or toothed, the curious eloquence
of those half-lives living in the lives they'd led,
ponderous as the stones that settle in the narrow
chambers of the unremembered past, surrounded
by the long-forgotten voices of their dead.

No Simple Truth

You say we need to keep things simple.
You declare that living's hard enough,
with all that we must try to understand,
the baffling cryptograms and innuendos,
the messy tangle of our circumstance.

The poet's here to say things straight,
you claim, that all her fierce enchantments
disentwine us from what's tied our lives
in knots. Her poetry's a blade we use,
you postulate, to slice through obfuscation.

While clarity's precisely what they're after,
I'll proffer poems harbor something else
as well, a sliver of reality, an abattoir of speech,
the steaming viscera of sacrifice at the altar
of precision, of divination and of dream.

Go seek the consolations of simplicity,
if the deeply simple's what you seek,
but run like hell from verse that cannot not
assume the shape of flesh, its gnarling surfaces,
the complex prosody of life devoid of purposes.

The Talmudist

invocation to Monsieur Chouchani

The particulars of a dream, we are told, what we remember of it, are nothing but the detritus of the day, the flotsam and jetsam used by dreaming to present itself to the wakened dreamer, to manifest itself, however absurdly, in the always dreaming eye. What is "happening" in the dream appears only to have an oblique connection to these manifestations, it seems, a perverse one in fact, like the logic or laconic pseudo-logic behind a bad joke. This perversity situates whatever must be happening in the dreamspace as not a thing beneath the dream, exactly, arising from the depths, but somehow off to the side of it, collateral to its voices and appearances. What appears to take place in the dream, parts of which we may think we remember on awakening, stands in a kind of apposition to the dream's instigation, strangely adjacent, always off to the side, outside the picture-frame of the manifest, of presence, insight and recollection.

I mention this because it is my own established role in life, my chosen profession, to sit here in this room and read, or perhaps more accurately to listen. More a listener than a reader, really, it is my peculiar practice to attend to the friable material of statements, declarations, utterances, what you might call that which is *said,* for fugitive evidence of the *saying* that animates it, a reality that lies somewhere else, that speaks otherwise than signification, yet always loiters in the vicinity, the proximity of the said. This practice, call it a vocation if you like, has gradually infiltrated my habit of thought, the way I see the world itself, how I am compelled to understand the Real.

In this light, world and dream cannot, I must admit, be clearly distinguished. I can only manage to see this world now, after long apprenticeship, the world we live and dream in, as a kind of jumbled text, the haphazard skein of references and interlacings that doesn't somehow manifest any form of "deeper" reality than itself, not something that arises from below, from beneath, as the evidence of primal laws or truths, but operates as a kind of vast elision, endlessly dendritic, that leads us all, its readers and listeners, relentlessly outward and away from every here and now, from the comforts of our cozy bench and lectern, this murmuring room to which I come each day to sit and listen.

And thus, my reader's life, my vain attempts to penetrate obscurity, to tease out the fine grain structure in our words, lead my attention always only away, away from fact, away from truth, into the speaking that's forever yet to arrive, encountered only in the disregarded circumstance, pursued along the roads that don't exist until my weary, scuffling, listening feet have formed them.

First You Must

First you must prepare to wait,
since waiting's what it's all about.
The unforeseen may undermine
your peace one day, or maybe not.
But should you even give a hoot,
make sure you're there to hear it
when it does.

Perhaps you'll somehow
know it by the sound it makes,
or maybe by the shape it takes.
You'll know it as an alien thing
and odd, the unrelenting feral
scratch, perhaps, of something
there behind the bathroom wall,
in the evidence that pesters you
with unimagined sounds and makes
its always dubious case
in logics not your own at all.

When once you've heard
that one true thing you think
you know about the world,
the thing it's always seemed
to say to you, then say it
often to yourself, rehearse
that strange unruly imagery,
this new unsettling noise,
and try to find its provenance,

the traces left behind, in all
the old familiar spots,
as if for you to find.

At some point you might just
regard yourself the author
of the thought you thought
came down to you from elsewhere
than your life, that you may set
it down in stone, in contours
or in words, in music all your own.
Then make sure you put it all in
every time, your one and only thought.
Say it fully, say it all,
say it each time out.

Ubi Sunt?

Where have all the readers
of Lautréamont gone off to,
who snatched a slice of Rimbaud
with their soup, a hefty hank
of Hopkins at the beach,
a dram of Ungaretti, Char,
of Kleist, Michaux, Cendrars,
Villon, or maybe even Valéry
or Yeats, Tsvetaeva or Dickinson
sometimes, to bed with them,
that such as these might
ease their minds to sleep?

How is it that the frosty parlance
of our narcissistic plainspeak,
the sounding brass of anecdote,
the homely unassuming homiletics
of a diffident sincerity, have muscled
onto center-stage? How is it that
we'd just as soon learn something
new about the world from a quick
perusal of the Classifieds,
or on the crosswords page?

And when exactly was it,
by the way, I cannot quite recall,
that melody removed its clothes?
Exactly when did poetry decide
to dress itself as prose?

The Interview

Yes. . . no. No, I never really managed to revise anything. There was never time. But yes, I suppose what remains out there, on the page, is what occurred, what occurred to me in its distant, peculiar way, and now remains more or less exactly as it somehow emerged, or better yet began its reticent emergence, but could never be said to have fully arrived. But yes, I guess it's all the product of endless revision, of the kind of life it had before being written, always what was on the way, never really finished, never quite arrived. No, it's more like some kind of precipitation or leakage, I'm thinking, something that has exceeded the limits of its capacity. As if the words were writing themselves. Not effortlessly, to be sure, maybe even painfully sometimes, but somehow independent of myself, of the efforts of any specific biographical, discontented me. And yes, the time of writing can always be assigned a specific instant or hour or year, but it is something more than that. Or maybe less. I want to say it happens in a time without duration, as if the words were already somehow there, and had been waiting there for a very long time, impatient, accusing me of a shameful negligence, an unpardonable delinquency. But no, no, there's nothing at all "automatic" about it, nothing remotely mediumistic, when words arrive. I am not somehow in their thrall. In no sense do I see myself as some well-tempered instrument carefully situated in the open window, poised to capture the transient breezes of inspiration. As best as I can describe it, it's when certain meanings, a peculiar meaningfulness that accompanies the words, that perhaps dwells in the sound of them, the sound they make in the mind, acquires a kind of weight or consistency, a substantiality entirely apart from their usefulness as mediums of communication, when meaning arrives like storm-clouds from somewhere outside the horizon of intention. And then a kind of exudation, a cautious drip, and the reluctant syllables seem to call for others, and then the cloudburst of the poem. And all I know is that I must hurry, that I am hopelessly late to the poem, and that this hurry is itself a hopeless thing, useless maybe, but somehow necessary, irresistible. And then there is just the road again, an unmarked path through darkness, into the past, and then, every so often, the startling unbidden presence of the words. And what results, what remains, what you are holding there in your hands, lingers like a scandal, an indecent hank of nervous tissue, a vital organ left behind, a wound that will not heal. So yes, I suppose that's all I've got for you today. And it will just have to do, and thanks for asking. I hope this helps in some small way. And regrettably no . . . no I suppose not.

II.
The Noise of Numbers

All there is
is number.
—Charles Baudelaire

Difference occurs in lightness,
in the airy, the affirmative.
—Gilles Deleuze, *Différence et répétition*

Time Does

When skating
down river
the sky in all
its possibility
passes.

Like chance
like circumstance
like galaxies your
thoughts collide
behind its voice.

Out west
of dawn dawn's
comets shake
their dreadlocks
in the dark.

Like distant music
in an ashen gown.
an anxious pallor
scatters silence
through the room.

Like all the years
like all the hours
like memory
and desire
things pass.

Calm down
be still
there's nothing
pressing nothing
to be done.

You needn't
flee needn't
ever even
move.
Time will.

Hic et Nunc

Zeno was asked the urgent question whether anything ever rests.
Yes, the arrow in flight rests.

—Franz Kafka, *Diaries*

Out in the surrounding air,
from nowhere in particular,
a musky odor of uncertainty
has nailed us to the spot.

The senses flare and reach
in each direction, southward,
westward, eastward, north,
where every gate lies open.

Yet we're somehow not
at liberty to choose a path
away from this, not knowing
if our frantic flight might lead

directly into this ubiquity,
directly toward that peril
waiting in the anxious open
where we'll no longer linger

in suspended animation,
out there where dire warning
flares, and dread, but where
all threat, for now, is future.

Yet time alone will send us out,
even as we're standing there,
out into wildness, into the open,
into light and into musky air.

Before Deciding

We will do and we will hear.
—Exodus 24:7

Early to the word,
released like breath
into the receiving wind,
the sky of which we're made,
yet late to the world,
we walk before thought,
the act enacted always
already before there's time
to formulate a theory
of action. We are
the flesh itself,
the tissue that
deciding is,
our incarnation older
than decision, our flesh
responding to the law
before it's given,
in a time much
earlier than hearing,
earlier than all judgment,
older even than belief.

Following the Law

> *No, said the holy man, it's not necessary to accept everything as true; one must only accept it as necessary [notwendig].*
> —Franz Kafka, *Der Prozess*

The law's not there to be obeyed.
It has no claim to truth. It's not
what's subject to denial, inviting
violation, but what we cannot fail
to bump against in darkest night,
in the retrospective light of day.

The law is all we're subject to,
the evidence of our subjection,
the trace of all that's powerless
in things, of what can't be reduced
to the cozy complements of liberty
and destiny, but what was always
there before we ever came to be.

The law is there where fascination
reigns, where what we cannot see
is also that from which we cannot
turn away, a land of cannot nots,
the doubled negative negating all
negation, older than perception,
a thing more ancient than cognition
or volition, older even than creation.

And though it's nowhere clearly
written, it never fails to make
a difference, and is in fact that
paradox that differentiation is,

where who I am is one who cannot
choose to feel or not to feel, a thing
all by itself alone, a thing complete,
that might remain indifferent.

The law is all we struggle to deny,
and yet this struggle's our awakening,
the birth of each uniqueness, not
a rule by which we can elect to live,
no truth that we can find or place
that we can occupy or flee, no calculus
of gain and loss, but the terrible
exigency out there that lives right here
within you and in me.

Adult Lullaby

You will not find its light reflected
out above the shifting deep or in
the cozy certainties of faith or in
the ringing declamations of the laws
and least of all the oracles of what's
been once forever written but only
there where contradiction lingers
in the wake of paradox and abject
disbelief where silence is the voice
of your response where wobbling life's
unsteady hand cannot lie still where
writing is the thing that writes and
just this ceaseless speaking speaks.

No Time

There's no law out there for you to follow,
no path before the passage of your stride,
no streambed laid to catch the roaring flood.

There's no time until the time you had
has passed, until your time is up; no time
except to cast a backward glance.

There's never Truth to find until the truth
has whispered in the blood, effaced each
foot-worn path, quelled this river's dance.

Concerning the Ineffable

You say there are no words for this.
You say it's all beyond description.
You see this strange condition
as your stumbling mind's encounter
with the indescribable.

They make of your predicament,
this muteness, a variety
of holy thing, and wish to see in it
what lies beyond, to hear in it
the cryptic hum of Being.

I say the world's an infinite, unshy,
relentlessly explicit thing, the elemental
incapacity of what's right here,
each complex artifact, its complex speech,
to not declare itself, to not appear.

I say the world conceals itself
in our plain sight, declares itself
in landscapes too familiar to be seen,
speaks always only to our deafness;
all art and science be my witness.

Land of Unlikelihood / Land of Unlikeness

This is a place
quite unlike any other
where each thing stands apart
where nothing seems to be
like any other thing
at all
sharing nothing
but the bristling atmosphere
of iron-shavings on a magnet
where everything's on edge
where watchful thought's
brought bolt-upright
in the uneventful night
by the whirring fans
that spring to life
without warning
in all the usual appliances.

This is no country
for those poets or taxonomers
who find sinuous connection
among the binding sinews
of the world
between the living
and the gracious dead
or who driven by eternity
raise violent objection
to the universal law of entropy

but for those who find
in all this evidence
of disconnection
abruption and disruption
the story of creation
and in defenseless flesh
the imaginary agency
the never-ending comedy
the unremitting urgency
of our unavoidable
and always less
than likely susceptibility
to communication.

In Dubious Terrain

And perhaps [Max] Brod recalled that he had scarcely read any text by his friend in which the impossible did not occur.
—Reiner Stach, *Kafka, The Years of Insight*

It is along toward evening, some people say, that the impossible tends to occur. Why this should be the case, no one seems to really know. Perhaps it is because the morning's vigor, the harsh verticality of noon, all the hallmarks of the possible world, are in decline. Daylight's rectitude has given way to a gradual recumbency, the slant light and torpors of evening . . . Yet the impossible, the occurrences that possibility has not paved a path for in advance, has no option but to occur. In its abject nakedness, the impossible is not the product of potential, of capacity or capacitance, not some latency awaiting release or a matter of choice or decision. The impossible must be (by definition, don't you agree?) that which is entirely without power, without the ability to be, and thus can only stand somehow outside the realm of what can possibly exist. It is an occurrence without the ability to occur, and thus cannot be anticipated. Or even remembered, for that matter. And so, "it" just seems to happen, you might say, this thing we call impossibility, somewhere in a quiet space to which we have no access.

But where exactly, you might justifiably ask, where in the geography of the existent, might such a place exist? Where do such events, in some comprehensible sense, *take place?* Where might such a quiet space be found, a world without power, a precinct of the real where what occurs occurs without the potential to occur, the way we say *"it"* is raining, a seemingly unconditioned, impersonal occurrence incommensurate with our capacity to anticipate or recollect? Right here, perhaps, if Kafka is correct, not just at evening only, but right now, everywhere, at every moment.

***

And in the waning light of evening, among the orchard trees, it was as if someone had thrown a switch to set the hillside junipers aflame. Horses filled the sky. Naked branches held their digits up as if to gauge some movement in the air, but quiet held its breath as if in anxious expectation. It must have been like this before creation (or so it seemed to him, the keeper of the trees), when nothing filled the world up with its waiting, when, in the splendor of those briefest moments before time arrived, the world of things was yet to make its appearance.

Products though we are of time and entropy, our senses seem to recognize these passive passing instants of creation, the silences we hear as imminence, of something nearly here or long past due.

We know this most when nameless trauma gathers in the brain, perhaps, as it was with the shell-shock victims Freud examined, like PTSD, when dread anticipation holds us in its iron grip, when injury incurred appears at the far horizon of our thought like something not yet here, a thing that hasn't happened yet, some thing from which, toward which, we hurry, an arrival for which we must prepare.

Yet by and by, for most of us, we who hold the poets in disdain, a gentle breeze arises in the sky, the branches gently sway, the gathered herds advance again upon the land. And in the end, time's arrow reasserts itself, and we are once again securely in the grasp of all that was and what is yet to be, insulated by our mighty capacity to recollect, to retrieve some misplaced fragment of ourselves from all that's past, yet reassured that what is past remains there in the realm of what's no longer here, anchoring us to this present place where we're released from noxious repetition, at liberty to join a future of abundant opportunity.

And yet our conscience harbors evidence of what is otherwise than being, otherwise than time as causal, linear, the neutral path of agency. Determined travelers along the road that leads from past to future, we are also, equally and inescapably, or so it seemed to him in that approach of evening long ago, particles adrift in a directionless sky, aliens at large in dubious terrain, creations of the never quite, never entirely past, fugitive animations of the glorious passivity, the impossibility, that whispers in the always dying light that we call nature, home, the world.

Of Paradox and Parallax

Hold Infinity in the palm of your hand
And Eternity in an hour
—Wm Blake, *Auguries of Innocence*

Distance brings all things together,
and sets them on collision course.
Notice how the distance we inhabit
nullifies the light-years said to separate
the galaxies, to thus abolish time.

Observe the way this trick of space
arranges all those lurid constellations
in our sky and gently places mighty time
at our disposal, installs its fiery avatars
within in the smallest gap between a thumb
and forefinger to gather countless eons
of creation in this soft prehensile flesh,
the modest orbit of our here and now.

Curious that such distance opens up
a way of seeing time as something
other than succession, as a dimension
that defies extension, as a curious
proximity in all the farthest things,
and unveils, in all that's most remote,
the perversions of duration, a time
that seems to take no time at all.

Curious that that which separates
all things brings everything together,
provokes a headlong inrush of the real,
unsettles all the consolations

that our bitter loneliness provides,
and sends us on a headlong quest
in search of blessed breathing room,
of time to spare, of some illuminating
interval, these tricks of space,
these illusions enabled, occasioned
by the fact of separation.

This Gay Science

We are on the brink of disaster but unable to situate it
in the future;it is perhaps already past.
—Maurice Blanchot, *l'Écriture du désastre*

The sky tonight
is no one's sky at all

no canopy or thatch
not hearth or home

no portents there
nor semaphors

for us to follow after
or ignore

but just what's left
of laughter once

we've stumbled
over circumstance

in the sparkling dark
and vast indifference

of our starry sky
its manifest disaster.

Archimedes Dreaming

Of the troublesome infinite

Oh God I could be bounded in a nutshell
and count myself king of infinite space.
—William Shakespeare, *Hamlet*

I took the measure of the world, or so I thought,
set forth the laws that govern what goes on out there,
between the one thing and the other, all those
permutations that obtain among the things that hang
as if suspended in a vast and neutral ether, illumined,
differentiated, by the space between them.

But lately I've begun to wonder, now there's time
for wonder, basking in the glory of achievement,
just what that silent tertiary term might really mean,
that space that separates some arbitrary *a* from just
another *a* we might call *b,* some version of The Same
whose differentiation's just a matter of position,
and just what might produce the logical entanglement
that any selfsame *a* might have with what is not an *a*
at all, the unspecific albumen, that ubiquitous *not-an-a*
in which each *a* appears to float and lie there anchored
to the spot, in which the self-identical is nothing
but a cipher, a place-holder, abstract, insubstantial,
replaceable, and infinitely substitutable.

What of this empty space that all my theorems require?
What is this constant medium on which those points must lie
and all my measurements rely? What incommensurate

relationship obtains between the object and its element,
between the thing and what is not a thing, no *b* out there
on which to set our yardstick or our compass, that thing
of infinite adjacency that stands this side of separation,
outside each *a* and *b,* outside all correlation, to constitute
each lonely little *a* as that which lingers somewhere far
beyond the arbitrary, as if uniquely situated, as though
specifically assigned, no simple candidate for substitution?

And in these musings, it's always me myself who stands
embodied as this tiny *a,* this thing alone outside of which,
positioned prior to that other *a,* is a thing without identity,
as if it were in contact only with the coiling serpentine
of time itself, and with this thought I sense my lofty
equanimity collapse, this Archimedean detachment
give way, to find me in an unfamiliar space where not
just thought but life takes place, where there will always be
another tale to tell, a tale of monstrous disproportion,
a tale devoid of all those old protagonists, my praxis
in amongst those stalwart levers, angles, fulcra, forces
and resistant mass, those sturdy *a*s and *b*s and *c*s, the tale
of what's outside us, just outside, immediate, not far
enough to measure, that's nothing other than the elsewhere
all around, an outside always there, an outside always in,
that inside-outness where the elsewhere's always here.

Yet No Ramanujan

I'll often find myself at large, it seems, adrift
among life's startling periodicities, witness to
a screen door's banging in the wind, captive of
some abstruse calculus involving coffee beans
or averages, the hapless prisoner of primes
or architect of rare, arcane notations, some
distant avatar of Le Douanier or Grandma Moses
left to marvel at the sly topology that governs
all my garden's fractious hoses, and imagine
I'm some tensile substance strung like jute
among the rambling, tangling roses, brooding
on these mysteries like a rusticated Euler, Gödel,
or al-Khwarizmi, a dazed observer standing
at the ragged limit of the Real, a stunned
provincial left alone upon the trembling scene
of this immense and mathematical event
we call the world, the awestruck product
of a whisker's oscillation in the feline breeze
of thought, a wandering particle without location,
an integer's commitment out of time, a creation
subject only to vibration.

Eternity at Twilight

The simple's said by some to lie somewhere
asleep within the mind, awaiting its awakening,
awaiting the arrival of that single simple word,
that single ringing note, that knowing glance, one
solitary spectral slice of light enough to open up
its abstract truth, a truth that sits somewhere
aloft this puppet-stage, this Punch and Judy show,
above the shadows of our sad St. Vitus' Dance.

And the copies of the things we lived among
(the way we were ourselves just copies, composed
of the eternal but corrupted by time, by the other
of eternity: pale simulacra of all that's real), all
realities lapidary, hard-edged and incorruptible,
never here but consisting of ideas headed down,
no bloom but the scent of it, no sanctity but its odor,
no death, no loss, but of the utterly dispensable.

I'm fairly certain, though, that that simple notion
of the singular, the idea of ideas, doesn't softly
sway there any longer at the bottom of the garden
as it must have done for you, Herr Socrates,
the way you thought you saw our complex lives
all fly apart (from the wide perspective of eternity),
to nestle snugly in the flinty unmixed rudiments
that hang somewhere in daylight's upper atmosphere.

And what you thought you saw out there, an abstract
world of forms where nothing new is seen to scamper
out beneath an abstract sun, cannot account for thought

or things these days, a world where all that is is always
new, where any one thing by itself is never just itself
alone, where there's no longer any height or depth,
but just what wanders here and there within our speech,
the depthless light, the broken syntax, of the complex.

On the One Hand

The single thing is not alone
unless the mind demands it,
is nowhere to be found
in song or shadow, nowhere
in the folds of sentient flesh,
the hungry verb, the soulful groan
of neutron stars, the propagating
surge of solitons, since all
of these are subject
to the endless winding-down
in things, the grinding work
and fissile consequence
of entropy (read time).

. . . unless it be our lonely
selves or primes, I hear you say,
and yet hang on there now, sit tight;
those dauntless efforts straining
to be nothing more or less
than one thing only,
only who or what they are,
are never more than
(don't you see?)
than monsters in the mind,
tautologies of thought,
bright visions of totality,
of adequation and identity,
that like all else are aggregate
and subject to division,
if only by themselves.

In Sympathy

I startled from a nap
in the easy chair of afternoon,
a book still open in my lap,
my achy shoulder hunched
and still asleep, and found
my left hand clutching
tenderly my right (as if
that hand were someone else's,
a child's, a lover's) with what
you might call something
like solicitude, concern,
affection, a gesture of support,
or as Kafka's diary records
in the early hours
of 11 November 1911,
when he too awakened
to find his left hand clasping
the fingers of his right,
some curious kind
of reaching out
"in sympathy."

The Everpresent Elsewhere

on transcendence

What is it anyway that you're
so eager to transcend? Transcend
what, exactly? The loamy scented
soil? the crystal sky? the sentient
pulp, the sap, the scaly, furrowed
mist? this nervous tissue's tingle,
its vibrant carapace of light?

Why is it that you feel you need
to seek, somewhere out beyond
the trillion trillion suns, some
meaning far more real than this,
this living space, these starkly
inconvenient truths, the elusive
breathing substance of this profuse
unmoored, eternally unfinished,
exceedingly material world?

Why is it you purport to find
within this world a world more
real than this, a bright adjacent
room in which eternity subsists
and writes the story of its truths
upon the flesh and stone out here,
and leaves its messages to drift
within this bright contingent
air of ours from where it calmly sits
upon its throne of higher power?

It seems to me it's really death
you seek, my friend, a happy end
to time and change, some compelling
evidence of what is terminally complete,
some consolation in the bloodless
silence of totality, a swift escape
from all that lies beyond you,
an exit from this life of infinite
diversity and mystery and change,
a deliverance from all that is, from
all these pulsing epidermal scenes
into the profound, the definitive,
the unmoved, unmoving, securely
rooted, cadaverous eternal.

Of Patience and Impatience

It doesn't exist, but only insists, consists, is.
—Gilles Deleuze, *Différence et répétition*

This restless world, the roiling universe itself, arises, you might say, from its boundless subjectivity and passivity. Perhaps what's there is only there by virtue of exposure pure and simple, of a radical vulnerability not reducible to deficient capability but to an incapacity *not* to be affected, *not* to be created, recreated, endlessly transformed. All matter, all sentient life, all perception and thought arises, perhaps, by virtue of exposure, in its being *subject to* the circumstantial, the unconditioned chance in which it improbably, infrequently, stochastically condenses, gasifies, solidifies, takes shape, animates, and assumes a place as if consigned to it, as if assigned a unique position, a location, a history. To a point where what you might call an individual character appears, something with a role to play, and at its most intense, an interiority, a singularity, a personality, the black hole in things we call identity.

But created how? Conditioned by what manner of intention or universal algorithm? This we always seem to ask, we who cannot relinquish our primal search for agency in the world, for causes and effects, for the melodrama of anteriority and posteriority, the unrelenting arrow of time with its befores and afters. And at the limit of our human speculations, some of us can't avoid imagining this awesome manifestation of effective power as a cause of causes, the intentions or caprice of an unconditioned Prime Mover.

Yet the path of all our sciences, all our human speculations, leads us inexorably out of the realm of agency, ever further into the realm of complexity, where what occurs occurs in an indeterminate space where qualities emerge from quantity, from number, from intensity, from the chance effects that arise and disappear like the fugitive patterns that show up here and there in the output of random number generators left to run at length.

Might causality be the final remnant of myth, the last gasp of those persistent mythologies that linger even in the realm of science? So perhaps indeed *All that is is number,* as Baudelaire wrote, arises in that space where *Even inebriation is a number.* All that is, it seems, arises not from a single causal something else, but the pressure exerted by the incommensurate, the massive disproportionality of what's other-than-itself, the unlikely and random world outside, exterior to identity, defying totalization, to what is not a self and does not in any sense exist.

All that exists is just perhaps the product of the autocatalytic system we call the world, a system that operates without in any sense being there, the consequence of an incapacity more fundamental than capability, than power, a susceptibility prior to Being, the complex entanglement of unmitigated happenstance and limitless improbability. Like stars, like galaxies, we are all here perhaps because we are *susceptible to being,* driven into being by an exigency that exceeds our capacity to hold fast, to remain at rest, within the nonexistent: each individual thing a random instantiation, an incarnation of number, of what we call physics, biology, slow time, all of us the offspring of the world's passion, its limitless patience.

Consider, if you will, this relentless patience of the world, its vulnerability, its passivity, susceptivity and exposure, its inability not to exist. And the eruption of our awareness as biological creatures, our inability not to be affected by the world that has created us, awakens us into the perceptible, conceivable world, a world susceptible to life as a kind of condensation, a curdling, like the stars and galaxies that interrupt the perfect blackness all around them.

So perhaps it isn't a surprise to find that our infinitely diverse inner worlds, our interiority and subjectivity, this individuality and irreplaceable uniqueness that we are, arrives always late to the game, constitutionally impatient, unable to stand fast and wait, hounded into consciousness, hurried forward in search of what has occurred, as Proust has taught us, headlong into a future that has already transpired, unlikely creations of slow time eternally in search of their past.

World as Passion

All that is, perhaps, or was or seems,
what hunkers, rattles, smolders, flares,
what slithers, skitters, drifts or strides,
what gathers at the knife-edge of the real
or hangs there like a teardrop in the dark,
is all that cannot just not be, the subject
of a subjectivity in things, no Being but
this being-subject to the world, this *patior,*
this patience all things bear, this passion
of the world concrete, the sheer passivity
that underlies each shining possibility.

Urgent Message to K2-18b

If we confirm that there is life on K2-18b, it should basically confirm that life is very common in the galaxy.
—BBC News Story

We've been busy pumping
dimethyl sulfide out
in frantic quantities
for centuries now, millennia
in fact, eons even, hoping
for a miracle, hoping someone
might happen on these
fleeting signs of life, these
signals of distress, hoping
this semaphoric chemistry
of ours might just perhaps
flag down some unobserved
awareness in the dark,
some compassionate survivor
of the need to live forever,
as she/he/they/it passes
through the neighborhood,
the robust product of diversity,
a post-capitalist creation,
as I envision it, emancipated
from our planetary plagues
of nationality, religion, profit
and disease, some lanky,
affable life-form possessed
of a life-expectancy just long
enough to make it here
(and back?), some sturdy
creature fit to make its way

across those light-years
to this place, whose ancestors
had somehow managed
to outlive the folly
of their species, the madness
of their race, and who might
speak to us of other worlds
out there like this, of what
endures, the jeweled nights,
the ozone sweetness
of their atmospheres.

Music of the Spheres

Behold the spherical, the ovoidal, the oviform,
how gravity prevails in all directions equally,
to draw the stars and gaseous planets to itself,
and fills the sky with curvature the way a berry
or a grape will fill the mouth, the way its jacket
pops between your teeth, the way its juices
jet across the tongue to fire the neurons tying
tongue to insula and onward through the frontal
cortex of your brain where shapes are stored,
and time, like gravity, holds each oblique sensation
orbiting across its deathless, delicate domain.

A girl I knew once served us a bewildering dessert
whose composition baffled me. I couldn't fathom
what those juicy semi-ovoid items were, suspended
in a frothy silken cream, until she said she'd sliced
some grapes in half, an act of haptic sabotage
that sent the tongue in search of likely analogs,
whose pulpy unfamiliar contours, blanketed
in lavish lashings of Cool Whip (of all things!),
resisted all my mighty powers of recognition.

Do those Platonic solids still hold sway within
the chambers of my brain? Is what appalled my pallet
lodged securely in the realm of all half-ovals now, in
some bisected form of ovalness that I can reconcile?
Perhaps, but it's that fluid sweetness I remember most,
the astonishment of bursting juice, the novel form
in which familiarity was cloaked that night, in just
the way that our familiar stars, though constant

in their tracks, observed up close reveal great jets
of streaming flame as if to stupefy with lurid
spectacles their excess and immensity.

But in the one specific case of flattened semi-
spheres afloat in jellied plastic spume, I won't
so easily be fooled again.

Animations

Turns out we're all
the likely product
of some transient
        in the prebiotic
        saline soup
        of early earth
                the vicinity of
                a proton gradient
                somewhere in

the neighborhood
of Godwanaland
perhaps perhaps
        some puny piezo-
        electric effect
        enough to spark
                an onset of com—
                plexity without
                the need for any

flashy lightning
strikes no cause
beside an instance
        of the impossible
        beside what's
        simply neighboring
                no mighty agency
                nor primal urgency
                besides adjacency.

Concerning Spirit

found among the lost notebooks of Ambrose Bierce

*spi*ri*tu*al adj.* Ghostly, not real, untrue [Lat. *spiritus,* air, vapor]

1. A term often correctly applied by enthusiasts of "feeling" to celebrate particularly vaporous works of music, the visual and plastic arts, and literature, intended as praise for qualities ethereal and indescribable, but just as frequently misapplied to artworks of substance whose perverse elusiveness, beauty and wealth of meaning must invariably elude cogent commentary, leaving only this one ubiquitous and triumphantly vague descriptor always available for knowing application by the tongue-tied commentator.

2. A term applied also to human beings whose hatred of the world in its manifest materiality prompts them to imagine "other realms and higher powers" out there in the ether above, or in some parallel realm alongside, this apparently disappointing one we live in.

3. A term in favor particularly among mystics, divines, art patrons, gallerygoers, table-turners, Romantics, vegetarians, aficionados, procrastinators, connoisseurs, society matrons, countertenors, sword-swallowers, transcendentalists, Neo-Raphaelites, mouth-breathers, millenarians, aesthetes, crystal gazers, ecstatics, Wagnerians, hypersensitives, neurasthenics, bassoonists, ideologues, enthusiasts of the sublime and rapt appreciators of every stripe, yet which has been found to induce a variety of unpleasant responses in others, ranging from mild nausea to intense moral, neurological and gastric discomfort.

III.
Of Interiors

Every person carries a room within him.
—Franz Kafka, *Octavo Notebook B*

Material Differences

God save the superficial world, the world
of surfaces and texture, the slippery slopes
of meaning, the buoyant melody of light,
from all that seems to beckon from the depths,
from all deep thinkers, all deep thought.

Write yourself a poem sometime, read one,
go to the place that puts you here again,
where each thing's strange again, where each
thing's new and every syllable conspires
with all the mute unspoken syllables out there,
and each solidity's composed of fire and air
and countless weightless, insubstantial things.

Observe the way this life we live,
the way each speaker's strange inflection,
can send us swerving in a new direction,
the way light bends off course, responding
to the feeblest gravitation, the way
we're drawn astray in search of what's
no longer there, as though in flight from all
our ponderous thought, as if released
into the accidental world, a world indifferent
to the crushing weight of our intention.

Just notice this, and put all images
of depth and latency and irony aside
to marvel at the vast sidereal night,
the slithering cloud and skittering sky,

the sideways scamper of your crab-like walk
through time, and wonder at this endless,
depthless universe itself, the affirmation
in its swales and swerves, the undulating
rumble of unceasing generation, and note
the world of difference it makes.

Fibonacci at the Tide-Pools

Every spiral thing's a fractal
of the fragile coiling world out there,
the whirling whorling world that two
successive numbers make, the curling map
that is this world itself, this Riemann's dream
of vast divergences, fashioned in the wake of
winding time, its algorithmic engine's
edgeless conch, this nautilus that spirals
on itself, this chiral shell of distances
we walk and wander on, the shiny surfaces
whose heres and nows are gathered
from each swept-up yesterday and day before,
each dawn the drawstring of its past,
each road ahead a road that's made of all
that's never really left behind, the breaking
light of each successive day that leads us
on through hope and folly, only ever
round and round, winding ever
outward and away.

Closer

Inaccessible but concerning, insubstantial but ineliminable . . .
the reality of a proximity which is not an existent.
—Joseph Libertson, *Proximity*

I am what's closer
to you than light
closer than air

closer still to you
than dream
infinitely closer

than what's there
than endless night
or crowding day

than what's just
in reach or right
beneath your grasp

closer even
than this you
that it approaches

than that you
who awaits
than the endless

patience it creates
of you by coming
ever closer.

Every Awesome Incidental

What is it happens in the rarest instants of attention
when, be it only briefly, the world itself, the substance
that remains outside the realm of self-concern, appears
to ambush your intention, to penetrate the pallor
you project upon the constellated surfaces of things,
to eclipse the sovereign searchlight of your reason,
if only for a moment, if only for an instant's season,
and in that briefest epoch will inoculate your thought
with what lies always outside thought, refractory
to intellection, and returning you to the immemorial,
to unfamiliar scenes you've somehow seen before,
into the wordless commonplace, the stubborn tug of some
specific thing will draw you from the reassuring shore
into the undertow of time, the buoyant seas of awe?

Approximations

Could it be that, in the belly of the night,
jerked awake by hibernation's tiny voice,
distinct, unrecognizable, feral, feminine,
by the sound your name makes in the dark,
your meticulous name precisely spoken
by the woman's voice, solicitous, emphatic,
you find yourself alone again, or not alone
enough, awakened to the messy aftermath
of your own concretion, to the dying echo
of that spontaneous ignition you weren't there
to see, location condensing into selfhood
in the cooling quiet, you the feral offspring
of immensity, of its procreating grandeur,
the stark enormity of what's not there.

. . . just as stardust gathers
in the whirling cradle of the void and kindles
in the winking nurseries of night, in the vast
indifference of a propagating sky, just this may
be the way our sentience flares, each instant
stoked and ceaselessly ignited by the wide
unfettered world itself, by all its chance events,
its births, deaths, thoughts, concretions, all
that rises and remains in the endless wake
of passage, products of no agency but
the noiseless flight of time, but the intonations
of your dream, by nothing present but what's
kindled into flame by the impossibly remote,
its bewildering intimacy, its disquieting adjacency,
its noiseless, faceless, ceaseless coming-near?

The Dreaming Dreams the Dreamer

One thing was certain. He wasn't ready. They were due at any moment, and nothing at all was ready. Everything lay in piles around him, but what on earth were all these things? Nothing familiar. Nothing he could recognize: clothing, stones, cardboard boxes, wheelchairs, the bones and antlers of ruminates, mechanical equipment of some sort, a clutter without logic, without significance. And above all, he thought, there wasn't anywhere to sit. Somehow, he'd neglected to acquire the sticks of furniture he'd intended to pick up somewhere, and of course something to eat, a bottle of wine, the simple courtesies his guests would have every right to expect. And those sheets of paper with the tidy rows of numbers they'd need to examine in their official capacity, all those numbers they'll have traveled all this way to inspect. Where on earth had he put them? He could picture them plain as day, those numbers, those reams of onionskin, grayish-white and slippery between his fingers, but where was it he'd seen them last? Where had he put them?

There had been plenty of time to prepare, of course, ample time, weeks, maybe even months by now, but somehow unaccountably he hadn't. And the long-anticipated hour of their arrival had arrived. And then there was the question of this bizarre getup he was wearing, ridiculously unsuitable for company, an emblem of his unpreparedness, open in the back like a surgical gown . . .

And then, awakening with relief into a world free from the threat of imminent arrivals, where no sheets of paper with absurdly long columns of numbers actually existed, where he was perfectly innocent of the criminal negligence that reverberated from the dream, where perhaps the anxiety it left behind, in its reluctant retreat, might somehow be compelled to reveal the secret of the dream, the key to its manifest untruth, he slowly drifted into a delicious, systematic, painstaking reconstruction of his blessed actual life, its happy prospects and routine pleasures, the little challenges he'd need to face tomorrow, in the fullness of time, things far too long delayed, to be sure, including (good heavens!) that urgent need to call home, which, as his pulse quickened, he remembered he'd had to put off for several days now. But why? Why hadn't he found the time to stay in contact? His family would be frantic with worry. His phone lay right there within reach on the nightstand beside him in the little hotel room. Panic gripped him. His heart pounded . . .

And then, in gratitude and relief, he awoke into a clarity that dispelled the anxious burdens of the dream. He knew its heaviness, its nagging aura of guilt, was nothing that need concern him now, that the morning sun would soon be rising, that in its light the comforting routines of his day would dispel this strangely lingering dread, this persistent grip of the unreal, the absurd inescapability of the absolutely not-true, and yet . . . and yet why this persistence of the silly dream, the grip of its its unreality more real somehow than the certainty of tomorrow's liberating dawn? How could something in the past, something that has passed, seem more present than the present, its unreality somehow more concrete than certainty? And down the winding pathway of these thoughts he drifted . . .

Until, awakening gratefully into the embrace of the familiar, into the sheltering darkness of his room, into the warmth of his cotton coverlet, soothed by the steady breathing in the bed beside him, he couldn't help but notice, as he slowly regained the composure that the dream had stripped away . . . didn't the location of the windows, the dimly visible furniture, seem wrong somehow? Hadn't things been oddly rearranged? Didn't everything appear to be elsewhere, closer maybe, than he'd left it the night before, nearer than it ought to be? . . .

It Dawns on Him

It’s what had gone
before I’d had the chance
to think, gone before
my thought had had
an opportunity to make of it
a thing familiar, another
me, my complement,
an object with a name,
an object subject to
anticipation, apprehension,
recollection, subject
to my scrutiny
or disregard.

It was, in any case,
a partial thing,
a partiality, a split,
a fascination leaving
something like distaste
behind, like apprehension’s
wake, or charm.

And its absence,
its residue, which seemed
a thing to think about,
the germination
of a thought, the onset
of a contemplation,
and a fleeting recognition
that the wake of it,

what it had left behind,
wasn't something only
to be thought about,
something subject
to my scrutiny, but
a breach that thinking
tries to fill, what's wholly
outside thought, the thing
to which our thought responds,
the sound of dawn, perhaps,
the outline of a tree,
an opened sky, a fracture
in the world that's me.

Regulus

The witnessing you are
is a life without decision,
your sight without the lids
you use to open up and see,
that choose to close or look
askance, behold, regard, observe,
discern, appreciate or stand
aside, or choose to back away.

The witness that you are
is not the one who comprehends,
and what appears is always more
than you can see, is something
more than possibility, darker still
than blindness, clearer still
than sight, a thing that lies there
far inside the wide capacious
reach and grasp of thought.

You are the lidless one who cannot
turn away from what you do not
care to watch, a witness to what's
nearer than this light, its presence
too immediate, its evidence a cry
too faint, its world a world
too close, alas, for sight.

En Attendant Galilée

Save me from curious Conscience
—John Keats, *To Sleep*

Conscience builds
itself a narrow room
of emblems,
commonplace
and passive participles,
from all the dancing
particles of thought.

Conscience dreams
eternity as infinite
extension,
as an open space
that lies outside
the narrow place
it knows as home.

Yet conscience sees
the room outside
as just another room,
a room a lot
like this one here,
a narrow thing, for sure,
but ever so much bigger.

Conscience situates
its slender oubliette
at the epicenter of the real,
that point from which
creation radiates,
where conscience wakes,
awaiting Galileo.

Incommunicado

If I cannot seem to grasp
what lies beyond my reach,
perhaps it's that I stand
within its grasp instead.

Perhaps communication's
just the sorry state we're in,
where each thing's not
out there at all, but nests
somewhere inside our skin,
where the outside's never
far enough removed
for civil conversation,
but somehow constitutes
the wobble that we are,
the flesh and bone
of separation, the state
of things before we were,
before the grasping mind
had made its lonely presence
felt, and had acquired
its pronounced capacity for need
and sorrow, its resolute,
distinctive taste
for poised appropriation.

Take comfort if you must,
and consolation when you can,
in the fact you're not alone,
the fact you're not positioned
somewhere far afield of things,

but there where contact's
just what's there, already here
yet never far away enough to see,
the voice of what is on the way,
its absence far too close
for comfort.

Prāṇa

Inhalations, exhalations,
each inspired breath's
an act of expiration.

The breath in every instant
articulates the drama
of the open wound,

connects and separates
and situates the breather
in its dubious terrain,

reveals the breather's
patience, her closure,
as exposure, as a breach,

and opens her to contacts
far too intimate for meaning,
to meanings more intense

than alphabets. At every
moment, there's this taking-
in what cannot be contained,

and every breath released
into the disproportionate,
into the incommensurate,

each exhalation, makes
of breath a precious gift
conferred upon the world.

Against Poetry

Georges Bataille's grave at Vezelay

I

Etna'd bared
its gaping wound
long before
your own time,
I am aware.
And while our stars
all smoldered brightly
in the smoky pit
of the sky
and down within
the blue meridian
of yawning earth,
we were never
quite aware
just what it was
that smoldered,
what it was, precisely,
that we didn't seem
to be aware of.

II

You were
the unlikely one
made useful
by the utterly useless.
Like Gorky
or Copernicus,
you arrived alone
and unannounced,
speaking only
the unspeakable,
naming only
the unnamable,
only those things
spoken from that place
where terror cannot
hide from ecstasy,
nor repulsion
from fascination,
nor tenderness
from cruelty.

III

Following you,
we began to darkly see
impossibility as our
necessity, as that
which cannot happen,
yet which must,
that all that cannot be
is just as powerless
to not, and began
perhaps at last
to dimly understand
that each interior's
the monstrous scene
of an intrusion,
the telltale evidence
of being's incompletion,
a violation that never
really happened
in any actuality,
yet endlessly returns,
eternally recurs upon
the ruptured surface
that's identity itself,
along the lacerated flesh
of what encloses

and exposes,
this realm of habit,
realm of the familiar,
this dubious terrain
where every sovereign
self enjoys uneasy
habituation, occupies
a habitation
without foundation.

IV

This was a place at last
of real specificity,
where any one thing,
every finite it or she,
each incompletion
of the wounded world,
and all we call identity,
is implication, the object
of those meanings
being always you
and meaning always me.

God Walks into a Bar

Actually, it was I who walked in. He was already there. How long had he been seated there, I wondered, in the darkness of a far corner, at the little table, nursing a little Cognac, wreathed in heavy pipe-smoke? I was late to the assignation, as always. He seemed unperturbed. At that time of day, it was the just the two of us, if you don't count the occasional squeak of a bar towel against the inner walls of the glassware that the proprietor stood polishing, endlessly, fastidiously, holding each piece up to the faint grey light that issued from the little windows up front.

He'd been happy to interrupt His schedule for my sake, or so He said, to indulge me in this little interview. It was awkward, to say the least, this conversation between someone without belief and Someone who doesn't exist. He readily acknowledged this latter point, I'm happy to report, the gorilla in the room, to be sure, this fundamental issue of His nonexistence. It relieved the tension I'd expected and dreaded. His cheerful concession to nonexistence broke the ice, and as I recall He seemed to focus on his status, above all, as a name. If memory serves, He was saying how the word, the Name, isn't exactly a thing, but something problematic that points, that offers itself, that "stands in the place of," like a sacrificial substitute for something, for all things perhaps, everything other than itself, and is never fixed in place, never firmly rooted, but always somehow on the way.

Nonetheless, after putting a few brief questions to Him that I'd prepared in advance, the heavy nimbus of Cavendish started to get to me. The cloud that enshrouded us seemed to be getting thicker.

I began to feel lightheaded and faintly nauseous, so I had to cut the conversation short, make my apologies, and hurry back out into the Autumn afternoon, grateful for the open air and the nearly empty street . . . yet, all in all, I'd say, the talk went well. As well as might be expected. I'd come away with what I'd needed, or so I thought, for the little article I'd planned to write. He said He'd be happy to meet up again any time. That if I ever needed to get back in touch, I could find Him in the book. I don't know. Maybe. The thing is, I've gotten so used to speaking with folks who, like me, seem to enjoy at least some form of existence.

But when I got back to the office, I was dismayed to find I couldn't make heads or tails of the detailed notes I'd taken there, dutifully, painstakingly, in the dim light of that lonely little bar. All that I'd hastily scrawled on the pages of my notebook was incomprehensible to me, back in the bustle of the busy office, as though a stranger had written them. In the end, all I had managed to come away with, as I think about it, was the sound His voice made. Something indistinct. Something wholly unrelated to the information I was after. An inhuman sound that attracted as it repelled, and somehow returned me to the world. The sound of a strange forbearance and an infinite patience. Something between a growl and a whisper.

Otherwise

To that which resists containment, no capacity corresponds.
—Emmanuel Lévinas, *Autrement qu'être*

How peculiar thought can think about
just what there was before thought was,
before our sentience and awareness were,
about the alien soil where consciousness
arises (and wherefore does it), yet we do.

We do because perhaps it's what we are,
in the end, because we're precisely that
which constitutes this desperate need
to separate, to stand outside the world,
to broadcast light upon a sea of objects,
on things to chase and things to flee,
the boundless threats and opportunities
there are out there, as if existence always
were the primal thing, upon that place
where Being seems to have a final word,
where thinkers firmly stand upon the solid
ground of thought, where our existence
isn't just what's thought about, but seems
to be what thinks.

Yet is it always so that we're content
to pull up short before the great enigma
Being poses, or have we also on occasion
stepped beyond that nagging question
to explore what lies the other side
of possibility? the evidence of what
each affirmation can and cannot
seem to say, beyond the laws of all
that may and may not be, and all

that animates the violence and power-
play that underlies these dramas of the self
and other, of identity and difference,
the endless comedy of chance
and consequence, illusion and reality?

I maintain we have done, and what's more,
we do it every day, as when we might
observe that consciousness arises
from the tidal flux of what cannot be
quite conscious, from that elusive element
in thought that makes us think, that slips
the mind, and so provokes the grinding motion
of our reason, or when we find capricious
quanta quietly at work within the energies
from which the matter of this swirling
world emerges, the world in which we live,
older than the one in which we reason,
a world we only might obliquely recognize
as ours, that lies outside the possible
and outside thought, where thought is what
responds to the appeal of that which isn't
always real, soliciting a recognition
refractory to comprehension, where identity's
that difference born of non-indifference,
this selfhood made of what's forgotten,
someplace far past seeing, something
far outside the limits of capacity,
more ancient in the end than being.

In Solitary

It isn't the room. The room seems fine, as rooms go, with its little window high up on the wall, the tiny sink, the steel commode, the sturdy table and chair, the shiny grey walls, the skinny mattress on its sagging springs. It might be as good a place as any for someone like myself, happy in his thoughts, *benign in my own company* as it says in a book of poems I once read. I'm at liberty here, in most ways, wandering in my thought, nested like an oyster in its pearly shell. No, it's the way the light seems to taunt me through that window, from under the door, a grey light mostly, without warmth. And the way the heavy grey walls, instead of damping, seem to amplify the anger that erupts in the galleries out there, the hoots and howls that explode in the oceanic, lamplit night that I imagine behind the door. It is, I guess, the impossibility of anything like solitude, here in this waking space, which makes me think *Solitary* is the last name you'd use for this situation of mine. Everywhere here, the dreadful irony of that word. It's not so much an exile, this circumstance, not so much the fact of my expulsion, this exclusion from the world, but the peculiar way the world seems to hold me at its absolute center, where I cannot manage to step back, to stand apart, where I'm subject to the smallest things, exposed to the narrowest light, to the pendant bulb in its cage, where I seem to be endlessly reoriented by the familiar, somehow altered and strangely destabilized by my unchanging circumstance. In the fragile stillness of my narrow bed, I can't escape the rasp of labored breathing. In every dream, the feathery, insinuating breath of isolation on my cheek, the licentious whisper of my absolute detachment, the undying echo of an unremembered judgment assigning me to this specific, unremarkable room at the unstable center of an indifferent circumstance, exposed to something more intimate than the violence out there, something somehow older than this separation: the rasping murmurs of a solitude without privacy, a solitude that never manages to find me simply by myself in this empty space, an isolation that doesn't leave me alone.

IV.
Among Others

The certainty of others,
the life, love, sight, hearing of others.
—Walt Whitman, *Crossing Brooklyn Ferry*

Bioenergetics

Cetaceans glide along the gradients
where planktons whorl and nightjars
follow moth-light through the dark
where hominins trail the moose and elk
along their branching pathways strewn
with sugars proteins enzymes fats
the stuff of which we're all composed
that each rapacious incarnated life
might seize and cycle through its eager gut
the substance of its circumstance and so
in turn deposit decompose return itself
to soil to air into the carrying dew
that carpets over all this ravening world
with opportunities and taloned threats
engenders all that we regard as picturesque
conceals in beauty what comes after you.

Muthos

I lie among your images
that are ravaged and burning
and masked in mud
—Vasko Popa, *Wolf Salt*[2]

They picked up the scent when he was still a few miles out. A scorching odor of musk and blood. Moving swiftly upwind, releasing little nervous yelps of dread, they found him in a clearing at the forest edge, caked in dirt and gore. Cautiously, they approached the three-footed king, converging in a snarling circle. Fondly, wanly, he grinned at them, the concubines, the pups, all his rival males, their fawning attitudes replaced by a cold fury. Coppery flame flashed from his narrow eye. Away from them for days, he'd left one mangled foot behind in tribute to the grasp of blue-toothed steel, the limits of his strength if not his limitless guile. As in a frenzy of confusion they tore from his frame the fur and furious flesh, it seemed they newly knew him as something more than just their leader, understood his presence as an intolerable, terrifying excess, and responded to his threatening powerlessness as if it were somehow both a hunger and a nourishment, an abandonment and an exigency, as something like a god. And knew the bloody stain of him upon their outraged jaws and throats and cheeks as something like a sacrament. These oblations, some say, the wolf now repeats with every kill.

At least that's the way I've heard it told. A silly story, really, rather childish and full of the kind of cryptic wonderment that childish minds enjoy. And perhaps this is just one among countless versions of the tale, as Borges might speculate. Perhaps in one of them the old alpha is merely driven out of the pack, and left to starve and die alone. In another, perhaps, he triumphs over all those opportunistic pretenders and reasserts his authority. In yet another he

---

2 Translation by Anne Pennington

might assume a subordinate role in the new hierarchy. And maybe this is not really a tale of wolves at all, when all is said and done.

A wolf is but a wolf, of course, like us all, in one way or another, a killing machine, focused impassively, passionately, on survival, nurture, anticipation and domination. No need for such fanciful nonsense as this tale of ritual blooding, its sentimental, pseudo-anthropomorphous implications of genetic memory and blind observance.

That none among the pack, in the wake of that strange day's flush of confusion and recognition, behaved in any way differently after the return of their alpha male then they ever had done from time immemorial, that nothing had ever really changed among them, become any less habitual, any more reflective, anything beyond what's characteristic of their kind, inscribed in their flesh, detached, however you look at it, by the passage of time from all presumable origin or cause, all purpose, all memory, all history; that much seems clear enough.

And with all this I must agree, but say what you will, in my imagination the stupefying appearance of the hobbled leader in the misty clearing's morning light, the terrifying spectacle of his weakness, his abject incapacity, will have sent a shiver of fear, a sacred shudder, something like awe, rippling through their nervous systems, traveling over the bristling fur of that startled, confused, desperate, quivering pack and outward into the indefinite, into the limitless realm of stories.

Seim Fronteiras

Sebastião Salgado's Sud Sudan

Biology is motion.
Its populous bodies stream
down avenues of least resistance,
as gravity requires, responsive
only to the grasping gravity
of circumstance,
swept through time by gradients
and tidal inundations,
the random consequence
of brief resistances
and impediments breached,
the migratory progeny
of infinite diversion, a substance
always on the move.

The life of bodies
is their unstoppable descent,
and endless deviation,
so what wonder that our living's
this eternal wander,
a dream of level ground,
ignorant of margins, built

to swirl unchecked past all
the most determined prohibitions,
defying all robust constraint
and every clever channeling,
and all those sovereign,
resolute borders, each stern
unbreachable barrier.

We say that is your place,
this is ours. Turn back.
Keep away. Flow back up hill.
Yet don't we know
that all our dire signage,
all our cunning engineering's
ultimately doomed to fail?

Don't we know that borderlands,
these arbitrary boundaries,
these feeble fictions
we call nations, can't restrain
the vital flow
of living populations?

The Exigent, The Inhuman

This responsibility is not an ability I possess, not an act of volition, but the significance of my inability not to respond.

—Emmanuel Levinas

                    The other person,
someone there that's just some other me,
is not herself, all by herself,
alterity.

                    And yet, arising
in the world outside the self, outside my
self, she signifies what can't quite ever
be familiar,

                    speaks to me
in muted tones of desperation,
in a voice outside proportion
with identity,

                    a carnal voice
refractory to self, to the nonself-
contradiction of the purely
self-identical.

***

She's a voice
from somewhere else, demanding
a response that I'm in no position
to fulfill, requiring

only, in the end,
that I awaken, and awakening this
awareness that *is* me, this peculiar
self I *am*, my scarcely

possible identity,
assigns me to this precise specific
place, informs me of an endless
obligation

that I can never
fully fathom, my obligation to all
that's alien in others, an obligation to
the disquieting

adjacency of the ab-
solutely Other. And as it penetrates
the barricades of my blithe
indifference,

exposes me
to what's exterior in me, the alterity,
the impersonality, that constitutes
this I I am, this self,

this unresponsive
me who's all there is of my response,
the one who sits outside capacity,
and only involuntarily

responds
from someplace out beyond compassion,
beyond empathy, beyond humanity,
to the supplications,

the countenance,
the indigent, exigent, inhuman voice,
the needful mouth, the soft surrendered
face, of the other creature.

Cost-of-Living Increase

Your death is nothing
you can call your own.

It's that one specific thing
out there you'll never

ever own, the wonder
of that dreadful thing

that isn't really yours
to dread except in the

approach of it, except
for that undying sound

you noticed long ago,
those noises left some-

where along the way,
the accumulated hum

of distant time, insistent
place, the loss of love,

the loss of face, and oh
the unrelenting absences,

the loss, that death, oh yes,
of course, of others.

The Spies at Canaan

> *The country that we traversed and scouted*
> *is one that devours its settlers.*
> —Numbers 13:32

What if this distance isn't something
steps can cross? What if what's remote
in things remains remote and won't
be brought up close by stealth or force?

The rooftops shimmer in the hazy light,
the Judean slopes that seemed not more
than hours away three days ago when
we received our orders, when despite

divine assurances we thought it wise
to trust but verify the providence
they say awaits us there, assess the might
of those who might oppose invasion.

But now, at three days out, I've begun
to wonder, since those spires and rooftops
don't appear much closer, just what it is
we need to know that faith did not supply.

And most of all I'm wondering how on earth
we'll manage to be worthy of that promise
made, survive intact a dubious chosen-ness
that grants us mastery and possession.

How shall this most holy destiny be served
without the killing and the being killed?
How might we keep this innocence alive
to witness every promised thing fulfilled?

Hungry Land, Silent Sky

It is not by accident that this journey, meant to be very short, became a long wandering.
—Emmanuel Levinas, *Quatre lectures talmudiques*

The explorers at Canaan brought to their mission a refined sense of justice. By betraying that mission, betraying their kind, they exemplified their kind as a people who cannot afford to rely on certainties, assurances, revelations, that cannot rest comfortably in the shade of the rights granted them by authority, by history, by identity. Their hesitation, the doubt that the explorers deposited in the minds of the people upon their return, was perhaps not borne by a sensible caution or practicality, but born of a nameless dread, the thought that to attempt to displace others in the land of their fathers, beside the graves of their ancestors, in the name of an ancient patrimony, would invite catastrophe. And most importantly, as suggested by certain commentaries, would oblige the people to sacrifice their identity as those who are never at rest yet who always, within the wide world of wandering, somehow remain at home, the home that isn't made of native soil but of a Book. (Although a book, you could say, that is always somewhere out ahead, always yet to arrive.)

It may oblige them to become just like the giants whose sandals they marveled at in the pursuit of a dubious destiny, and to eventually resemble those devouring, rapacious, seemingly settled others, seeing in one another nothing but grasshoppers, seeing all others as an inconvenience, an impediment that must give way to what's theirs, what's written, to the rights and stewardship granted by a higher power, by what speaks from the mountain with the voice of mountains, an immensity beside which we creatures in the here below are as smoke, as nothing.

So what they doubted was not perhaps just the practicality of an invasion but its consequences for the people, for people full stop. What they doubted was the authority (read legitimacy) of their marching orders, the imperatives spoken by the prophet and the god, for after all, prophets and gods will only ever speak to us in the imperative. Thus, their final report, insidious, intolerable, treasonous, had without question to be discredited and excoriated over the ages. No wonder, since their debrief resulted in a 39-year delay! Yet somehow perhaps, by discrediting the divinity of their mission, they had sought to preserve intact the sanctity of its inspiration.

And so the horns of an intractable dilemma. And these scouts (with the exception of Caleb and Joshua), no surprise here, have been roughly treated by the Talmudists and other commentators over the centuries. They have even been accused of departing under the cloud of an agenda, long before returning with one. Yet surely it was the righteous Joshua and Caleb who carried an agenda in both directions: namely their faith, their beliefs, their certainty that promises made would be promises kept, and that milk and honey would flow for the people. Their fellow spies, patriarchs all, notables, heads of families, gathered the evidence, as directed, and brought it back. All that plump, heavy, syrupy fruit, along with tales of awesome fortifications and a race of giants.

Like practitioners of the sciences or arts who wander out into harm's way, into dubious terrain, under a voiceless sky, those who dwell at the probe-ends of knowledge and understanding, these explorers presented their results without valorization, took their own positions with regard to the significance of that evidence, and left things for the people to decide. Such perhaps are all reports carried back into the realm of righteousness and certainty by the explorers of a barren country, by scouts who infiltrate the provident valleys, the mighty cities, every landscape of the future and dream of the past. Such are the unprescribed findings of poems, you could say, of experiments, conjectures, all the "essays" presented in constructs of sound and stone, line and color, all exploratory accounts of what we call meaning in the world.

In their fidelity to fact and freedom from intention, these all expose themselves to accusations of insidious betrayal, of violating the common cause, disregarding the explicit agendas of their kind, admitting hesitation, casting doubt, speaking as if in foreign tongues of tiresome alien interests, speaking indistinctly from somewhere outside our accepted logic, expressing a humility, a humanity without rights, a humanity that exceeds itself, a humanity that lives always elsewhere than in its rightful home, left to wander at liberty out beyond the bounds of righteous self-interest.

So why should we be surprised when our explorations, these godless, senseless, incoherent reports, are met with a kind of embarrassed silence, suspicion, incomprehension and distrust? Why be surprised when we know full well that the accounts brought back from the outer edges of familiar logic harbor unsavory news requiring new vocabularies, disbelief, the acceptance of impracticable consequences and unearthly responsibilities, even perhaps new understandings, however unpalatable, of what it is, exactly, this burden of the human?

The Misery Machine

Marx in the library of the British Museum

I really don't begrudge the dream
of those who conjured up and realized
the comforts of this place, the warming
welcome of a morning chair, the ample
room this luxury affords, the luxury
to gather within easy reach the heavy piles
of books and manuscripts, the Erzgebirge
of my craft, the precious ores this lifelong
miner's work of mine requires.

I don't begrudge of anyone the jollity
of bindings stamped in gold, the ranks
of unread fascicles ascending from
the intricate terrazzo of these polished
marble floors into the dizzying vaulted
ceilings of this space, the light-filled
openness of all its rooms, its atmosphere
so distant from the cloying dampness
and eternal gloom, the unabated chill
and endless torments of our tiny drafty
rented rooms at 28 Dean Street, Soho.

I can only marvel at this boundless
battery of oak and stone, the oak alone
enough to launch ten heavy-canvassed
Fighting Temeraires, the raw materials
and workmanship that privilege,
rapacity and capital affords.

The precious substance of my labor here,
the purpose of this passion, after all,
is only to reveal the sly eternal link
by which economy is joined to politics,
the way that riches must accumulate
where power lives, and grow unchecked,
this excess that the wealthy reap from time
and skill and labor purchased cheap.

And if, as I predict, the laborer
must one day rise to claim his share
of all that he creates, it's not that we
must lay to waste such comforts
as surround me in this room, but only
that our abundant lives be made aware
much more of misery, and made
to understand the way our cozy
bourgeois world's arranged in such a way
that someone else's misery's required,
the way within each rare commodity
that decorates our lives a faceless
unnamed misery resides.

Our abundant age cannot deny itself
such forms of self-congratulation
as this grand house affords, the soaring
odes to empire and prosperity that adorn
the mercenary streets, the surface treatments
of its boundless conspicuous contentment.

But it has placed its gaudy monuments upon
the fault lines of history, or so I say, its noisy
celebrations all but deaf to the rumbling
of a vengeful discontent more consequential
than all our proud Trafalgars, heedless
of the seismic tick of mankind's clock,
the hour set to menace all we think our might
has earned, the trembling thing that underlies
the bedrock of our tenuous foundations.

I trust my diligent archival excavations,
my own exacting labors in this palatial setting,
sheltered gratefully for a few hours each day
within this soaring masterpiece of civic self-
congratulation, might inspire at least
some form of moderation in the conscience
of my reader, at least some earnest recognition
of the fact that what we all enjoy is not enjoyed
by all, that this untidy scrawl of mine,
this waxwing's nest of dense unruly pages,
might call us to some action in the service
of a future time where just proportion reigns,
alongside beauty and abundance, in every
humble home, in every heart, on every street,
at every meal, down every common hall.

In the Company of Sharecroppers

images of Lange, Bourke-White and Walker Evans

There is no refuge from the one
who doesn't see you. Is this unsettling
blindness in each subject's milky eye
the expression of a native wariness,
a deep distrust of the camera's dark,
dispassionate, cyclopean stare, or just
the unmistakable evidence
of a profound indifference?

No sympathetic scrutiny
can ever quite decipher what it is
about these sculpted geologic faces
the photographs convey,
the countenance in each that aims
its alien gaze somewhere way out past
your fawning deferential shoulder
to focus its attention somewhere
in the fleeting moment's faraway or out
among the furrowed fields of time.

We're made to marvel
at such dignity as this, the angular
eloquence of wrists and knuckles
jumbled in repose like hoes
and rakes and trowels left to rust
beside the shed, each unselfconscious
digit's spatular nail so pinkly tidy,
each monochrome a study of neglect,
of endless fruitless jobs of work;
each gathered limb an essay
in unselfconscious elegance.

Between that hand and yours,
at rest upon the smart precision
of the glossy page, the distance
of a hundred years. And yet
the slackness of your speckled wrist
betrays like his or hers the work of time,
the way life bends us to its will
and writes upon the surface
of our skins an unforgiving narrative
no narrative can quite reveal,
no narrative can ever hide.

From the lustrous surface of these pages
each glistening brow, the shadow
of a hollow cheek beneath
the cheekbone's jagged outcrop,
harbors all the interlacing furrows,
all the scars that work and worry wore,
betrays in each a tangled maze
of unabated bitterness. Yet even so
a kind of fundamental kindness
kindles in the weary bloodshot gaze,
disguised as resignation.

Later on, at the bathroom mirror,
somewhere in the private interval

between audacity and shame, you try
to catch your own eye unawares,
but there's nothing there to catch off guard,
no story much worth telling, nothing
furtive underneath the papery lids,
no occasion for surprise or vantage
to subdivide the seer from the seen.

It's not, I guess, that mirrors lie,
or worse, that mirrors always speak
the brutal truth, and not at all that they
might just incriminate their beholder,
those haunted, haunting images that drift
incarnate through your book, the majesty
of someone seated in the ancient shade
of a blinding afternoon, but that the life
that speaks in those obtusely angled limbs,
in all the haggard faces of their distant world,
obey the universal logic of a place you're not
equipped to recognize, yet linger nonetheless
like riddles in the mind, like the cryptic axioms
of a lost geometry, like magnitudes unthinkable
in that privileged space you've known as life,
the surroundings that this brash, inquisitive,
impertinent, this prurient gaze of yours,
might easily identify.

V.
Past and Presence

Time slogs my bones to ash.
—Eric Fisher Stone, *The Drowned Phoenician*

After the Dark

In my mourning you appeared
a mournful thing, full with pity,
gravid, distracted, nurturing that
novel weightlessness beneath
your gown, your bridal veil
of cobweb, ash and weeds,
your dignity arrested in mid-stride,
en route to somewhere else
than here, somewhere far outside
any other here.

As time saw the flaming pain
of it subside, the windy violence
grow quiet, the cold stone gently
settle in the gut, I sensed the pity
that was there give way to a delicate
insouciance, something akin
to gaiety, you might have said,
the unearthly demeanor
of a half-life, the unhurried transit
of an excess over presence.

Like the mantis, all but motionless
at the screen, you moved along
with the scandalous indifference,
the haughty languor, of one long gone,
of one no longer one at all,
the velocity of what's no longer there,
of one not merely, not simply, not only,
but yes, how absolutely, gone.

Cap d'Antibes

The sun is hot, the sea stupidly blue . . . a pebble, a blade of grass, the line of a hill . . . can help me. Not to understand, but perhaps to know.
—Gisèle Celan-Lestrange to P. Celan, April 2, 1966

Turning from the torpid, ponderous, passive,
stupidly sparkling sea, its vast recumbence
far too large for meaning, into the cloudless
sailing altitude, into this bluest breath from out
beyond the palms, the rooftop tiles,
the streaming quay, the tidy little port,
the car fumes settling in the narrow streets,
into this breath released at last, this breeze
that gently puffs the collar of my open shirt,
that slips across my skin to open, open me again,
to extricate from vivid recollection
all my graven images and fond imaginings,
the beloved imprint of your Janus face,
all the remnants of a light too stark,
a universe too large for meaning, into the breath
that lifts me once again away from empty
thoughts of time and space, away from death
and into specificity: this stone, this blade,
the harshest heat of breathing day.

Under the Influence

Evenings, luxuriating in the glow
of our Tanquerays and mezcalitos,
the dreamlike haze of dust-jackets
and blue walls, the filmy shadow
of the festive light he cast on things,
how gingerly we'd place each record
on the silver spindle, set the needle
gently down and watch it glide
into that miraculous vinyl groove
beneath the breathy panpipe whistle
of concentration on our lips.

And how we awaited his reaction,
his surprise at that prodigious selection,
his appreciating response, his delight,
his infrequent fulsome praise.

But it was all too often otherwise:
A bit neurotic at this early hour,
don't you think? Let's have some Monk
or Hendryx now instead. We'll save
the Ayler for much later.

Pale Penumbra

for J.L. in remembrance and sorrow

That shadow seemed to sit beside him from the start,
like a storm-cloud or a pair of black silk pajamas,
jocular, laconic, intellectual, so close beside him
you could almost hear its chuckle in his words,
the way it seemed to filter light around his frizzy head,
the turbid meanings in his voice, the emphasis he gave
to certain harmless syllables, the caustic wit
that glimmered greyly in the eye, the coruscating grin
enough to strip the varnish from the filmy surface
of a thousand lesser lights.

It was indeed a world of lesser lights we'd managed
to find refuge in that year, the year I ran headlong
on that wall of his. Once I told him that he'd been
the ruin of my academic life, and its actual beginning.
And sure enough he was, as it turned out, the making of us.
He'd swiftly dropped the dime on all that we held dear,
and we'll not forget the ring of it, the way a world
within the world we'd known had opened up to send
us scrambling down the stony path behind that voice
of his, behind that bouncing shadow.

In the end, the world would have its way, he'd said,
and how the world he knew so well had managed blow
by blow to knock his stuffing out. And in the end,
the painfully protracted end, the shadow seemed
to take up residence within, as if all he'd had to do
was step into its emptiness, or see it slowly seeping
through the emptiness in him. No longer that idling,
companionable phantom we had known, in later years,
like time, it was what he'd come to harbor underneath
the skin, the weary vestige of a guttered flame,
the smoldering substance of his absence,
and was never seen again.

Seminar Table

Levinas at Hopkins, a story second-hand

All the lively talk abruptly stopped
when he appeared. The chairs
scraped back. We stood as he
walked in and took his place
at the far end of the long oak table,
motioning us to sit. He quickly
doffed his coat and hung it
on his chair, and seated, carefully
rolled up his sleeves, uncovering
those grave-digger's arms of his.

He then removed his notes and watch
and set them side by side, while all
the while those smiling eyes that filled
the smiling room swept round and caught
and held the smile on every one of us,
upon those fond involuntary emanations
of our long-anticipated thrill.

Compact, burly, built in the timeless style
of the proverbial brick shit-house,
he seemed the very image
of your local hometown butcher,
leaning over all the shanks and cutlets
of his exacting, kosher, sanguinary trade.

I cannot quite recall the sound
his voice made in the room that day.
(He spoke in French. His English wasn't
all that good.). All that lingers in the memory

of the day is the silence gathered all around
his words, the silence that his audience
made as each one held his breath, the silence
in those sounds he left behind, and somewhere
in my head it says that, for that while,
it was as if no finch or oriole or towhee
sang out past the open windows.

He started with some verses of Corneille,
of that I'm sure (*Corneille, imaginez!*),
and startled us with what came next
and after that and after that, reiterations
of a thought that lapped upon the shores
of understanding like an ocean, in waves
that scoured those landlocked academic
minds of ours and hung us out to dry
like so much meat suspended from
the meat-hooks of that quiet seminar
in the genteel paneled room, arrayed
along its oblong chopping-block,

. . . yet also somehow soothed us
in the presence of his courtly *politesse,*
his unearthly ruminations, the meticulous
dismemberments, the savage ethic
to be read in all this problematic liberty
we share, our unrelenting responsibility,
the penetrating *Menschlichkeit* that resonated
in the voice and augured in our minds,
the bloody leavings scattered on the floor
of that galvanic room, his oh so tender abattoir.

The Unnamable

a Bullsnake elegy

He's a paragon of rectitude. Like spiral time,
he has no reverse gear. *Agent provocateur,* creature
without guile, he turns up only when we least suspect.

Emissary of innocence in a world without dimension,
he's a line from here to there, a length, however long
in life, that thought makes always longer.

At the threshold of confusion joining intellect to dream,
the indistinct horizon basting earth to sky, he occupies
the speckled borderlands of fear and fascination.

He's the visitor, the visited, a slender reticence
without intention, a universe of noiseless repetition,
a scandalous appearance in a time without extension.

The evidence of endless questions, persistent source
of absent answers, he's what linearity conceals in light,
an uninvited vagabond with nowhere good to hide.

Yet funny how his image and this coiling syllable
his name (dreadful as divinity's), can strangle speech
and startle blood like the sudden passage of a god.

The Birth of Distraction

toward a unified field theory of adolescence

His scattered image seems to dance
across the screen of recollection like a puff
of pollen, blade of grass, or curl of smoke,
as if the softest breeze of memory might pass
clear through his narrow frame. As though
he'd never been, but through the passing years
remained the object of our endless speculation,
while we in fascination watched his profile fade,
contract, dissolve itself in pure stochastic motion,
into a senseless Brownian quiver, to linger only
as some shapeless protozoan thing, a life-form
made entirely of roiling soup and membrane,
a gathering of awkward flesh that feels its way
in darkness through the tidal streams of innocence
and happenstance and blithe indifference.

Indifference, was it? Or maybe just uncertainty,
or better yet perhaps it was a simple matter
of distraction, the abstruse mechanics of a life
unsettled by the ache and surgings of its youth,
its yearning melodies, the ubiquity of its desire,
the bareness of imagined thighs beneath a saucy
dirndl skirt, the fulsome bloom of countless
carnal revelations, all the lively décolletage
and joyfully symbolic spectacles of Spring.

Life lay long before him then, an abstract thing
he'd have to reckon with from time to time,
yet softly time began to limn its imprint
on his gait, to sculpt the peerless contours

of a face, construe the geometric axioms at work
on teenage limbs at rest, reveal a novel timbre
in his speech, as if this all were just the evidence
of an instar's graduated birth, a miracle
of individuation, a map to show the winding path
we take along the road that leads each one of us
from illusion into disillusion, the way we each
must steadily, painfully, impatiently, alas
eventually, adolesce.

The Price of Succeeding

for Eric Ormsby, il miglior fabbro

As life cuts every distance short
to offer up what once seemed far away,
and place within your easy grasp
each prize that led your life astray,
you'll find what seemed to beckon
from that world beyond your reach
has shriveled to a paltry thing,
all luster lost, the lifeless prey,
the ashen aftermath, the empty
consequence, of firm possession.

Wise folks will tell you that it's really
you that's changed, that you're not
anyone who wanted this, that now,
with all the world laid at your feet,
the yearning one you were is gone,
that who you are is only someone
time has left behind, time's orphan
left to wander onto open ground,
a nameless grief that seeks in vain
the long-familiar contours of desire,
the comforting horizons that once
meant home to you, your erstwhile,
long-departed, yearning self.

Post Mortem

Sometime after three in the morning, he died of worry. He never saw it coming, and it took him a while to understand what had occurred. He'd never really worried about the possible, the universe of things that might happen, but only, endlessly, about all that had already happened. He considered himself their cause, these things about which there was nothing left to be done. And yet, ridiculous as it seemed, his thought struggled to find ways to reinsert itself into the orderly stream of causes and effects. Thought itself (a kind of residue, it sometimes seemed to him), the brute fact of consciousness, was only life's untiring attempt to transpose its past into a future, to occupy a place of decision and perspicacity, a commanding perspective that gazes out upon a land of infinite possibility. But in moments of astonishing lucidity, he'd see the deathless persistence of his so-called life as a world of accomplished fact, a product of the said and done, of the unchangeable, the impossible, filled to capacity with what was, what has been, leaving no room for action, no room for anything but this impersonal concern, this unquenchable urgency, this undying regret. As his death began to dawn on him, he realized there was nothing to be done about it. He understood that it had somehow always been there, in the past that stands beside each present moment, immovable, unavailable to decision, refractory to all initiative, indifferent to action or decisive inaction. And so, without options, he continued on as he always had, continued on as usual.

Time Past as Obligation

What's left unsaid, what's left undone,
a world unfinished, arrested mid-sentence,
abandoned breathless in suspended animation,
draws all the carefree present moments
into its domain and demands my full attention.

Unlike you, I seem uniquely unequipped
to let it go, as it cannot let go of me. The further
down the road I seem to get, the more I wonder
at the strange tenacity it has, the way
its long-neglected voices follow me.

In dream, the dreams that dream themselves to me
accuse my dreaming nights of some neglect,
some oversight or crime or business left unsettled.
Perhaps it's just the way time circles on itself,
a peculiar power the powerless alone can wield.

CR101

Out in the middle of The Fence's yard
there's a solitary ditch-fed spruce,
transplanted from some distant elevation,
hauled here long ago into dubious terrain,
that stands these days superbly unaware
in the weedy detritus of its abandoned site,
among syringes, cans and cellophane,
beside the ditch and charred remains
of that notorious fence's house.

He was the guy to go to, so they say,
the guy who paid hard cash for anything
in urgent need of moving fast, the spoils
of last-night's raid, the smash and grab-it,
the baubles left beneath a bedstand lamp,
be they gemstones, be they paste, the *lana*
you would need to feed your hungry habit.

One night some rival torched his place,
the very night that we ourselves moved in,
we transplants from our sundry elevations,
to an old adobe down the road. And so
we never really knew how it had been,
that corner lot before the conflagration,
the way that adolescent spruce tree stood
before it grandly rose up through the years,
a monument to its resilient neighborhood.

Life accumulates beneath the cumulus
that gathers on the towering peaks to drift
like smoke, like blue fog climbing upward
through the mountain passes, nestling
into all the valleys that shelter in the shadow
of these peaks, their towers vertical as pines,
their pines as dense as circling starfields are
in whirling transit through the howling night.

In waking dream, when that majestic spruce
stands blanketed in snow, I wrap myself
in weavings from the grizzled wool
of sheep that graze up here in Truchas,
Trampas, Chimayó, to cross the ditch
and sit out there beside that brash defiant tree,
and come to terms with all that brought
and keeps us here, the curious grace
that somehow led us to this spot, this land
of quiet desperation, land of pain, this blessed
refuge, scene of violence and peace, this *hortus
deliciarum,* that spruce's dubious domain.

Apart

On a modest hill
set among arrogant trees
this house sends
shoots aloft and root-
hairs out to meet
the lazy circles
bustards make
out past the contrails
left by Harris Hawks out
past the wake of ravens
the delicate traceries
and lacework products
of our scratching wind
the muddy light
beneath the lake
below the moon-
soaked streets
out back
of what's behind
the howling world
a place apart from all
that gathers to itself
that piles up covets

possesses acquires
away from all those
clear-eyed optimists
and pessimists
out past all hope
and hopelessness
a place though
wonderfully composed
like everywhere a small
defenseless place
an insignificance
and helplessly
exposed.

Through Life's Mountains

to a Basque walking stick

The gleaners found the limb you were
and scarified your tender Medlar bark
and left you for a year or more
before returning with their shining saws
to appreciate the wander of your scars
and cull you from the leafy shadow
of that quiet hillside grove its woodland
tilth the forest floor's decay the sturdy
trunk the conduits of cambium from which
you'd suckled sap and gathered through
the thirsty stomata of your leaves
the nitrous gift of mountain rain

. . . and took you down to dry and brought
your native curvature to heel that in
your varnished rectitude adorned
with polished bone and scalloped bands
of silver wrapped in braided strips of hide
you might come home to us where you'd
have pride of place to one day (wild *makila!*)
and wander out again perhaps among the wooded
slopes where you once grew where we
like you our stout companion and support
might feel the breath of life within
the breathing mountain air against
the time-scarred surfaces beside
the long-healed lacerations
of our dimpled time-worn
sunlight-varnished skins.

After the Squall

Out here the pitch-dark branches
of our startled trees release fat drops
in the aftermath of a sudden squall
while winter holds its breath beneath
the ashen bunting of a low-slung sky

and I'd swear I've just awakened
in the bracing climate of some
altogether foreign place a forest
somewhere consummately north
of here a forest outside Bergen

to be precise and in the interest
of precision too a melody of Grieg
arises from that rain-soaked path
a melody of long-forgotten shade
beside the quiet lake at Troldhaugen

a song that whispers in the bitter air
that pricks the bracing moisture
on my cheek (for never is the source
of such impression merely vague
this odd persistent presence

of the past in us the curious
twitch of time that lurks uncorked
within the muscle and the mind
and mostly disappears before there's
time enough to accurately recognize

its provenance) until the fading strains
of *Morning Mood* or *Wedding Day*
have yielded to the keening wail
of *La Llorona* on the hill the flapping
shawl and unbound hair that in this

rising breeze will reassert itself among
the sandstone ridges of our elevated
desert place because the actual must
muscle out each transit of a fragile past
to ever in the end unfailingly prevail.

Radio Nights

for Patti and Eric

They'd hired him on the spot, after a few brief questions. Questions that seemed strange to him now, but which the state of his nerves that afternoon had made it impossible to focus on at the time. Like, "Do you own a car?" And then it didn't really seem to matter that he didn't, that when he replied "No, a bike is all I seem to need. I ride my bike everywhere," the conversation just moved briskly on to another non sequitur, like, "I see. And, um, do you have a life-partner? Any children?" None of it seemed to have anything to do with his qualifications or preferences in music, which was the occasion for the interview, his suitability for the role of late-night disc jockey at the station. But his answers must have been adequate somehow, not shamefully disqualifying, as he'd feared, because here he sat, gainfully employed beside the long boom of the desk-lamp, in this tiny control room, his reflection in the window separating him from the darkened studio behind it, surrounded by turntables and disc players, the dangling, intimidating microphone and all those knobs and dials and glowing meters, most of which he didn't dare to touch, not knowing anything about what they were to be used for.

And he never saw them again, those interviewers, up to now at least. They'd asked when he could start. "Midnight Friday okay? Be here ten minutes early. Betty will show you the ropes." And Betty was there, just as they'd said, to point out the five or six important buttons and dials, all he really needed to know, along with the four or five power indicators and volume meters. He'd usually pass Betty in the hall on his way in, three nights a week, proverbial ships in the night. Otherwise, he never saw anyone at his place of work except the night janitor whose presence, round about 2 am, mostly, was announced by the sudden flick of a light switch outside his window, the abrupt disappearance of his reflection in the glass, a hasty circuit of wastebaskets emptied, a quick mop-up, some purely ceremonial flourishes of the feather-duster, a perfunctory wave, never a glance in his direction, and then the room beyond restored to darkness again, the abrupt return of the mirroring window, the echo-chamber of his workspace, the sense that he might just be the very last person left on an empty planet.

But his concern about the interview's vagueness was probably unfounded, considering the good possibility that no one out there was listening to these peculiar selections of his, at this late hour when most of the city had retired for the night, where these broadcasts were a kind of placeholder, he figured, to keep the signal alive over the six hours of his shift.

And sitting here surrounded by stacks of vinyl he'd brought from home, he'd marvel at the good fortune of this dream job he'd landed, quite improbably, where he was free to send out into the ether all the sounds he liked best, each evening's broadcast carefully selected, sequenced, meticulously curated, designed to reach that specific kind of audience of which he was perhaps the only breathing member.

He'd often just start with sounds, like whale song sometimes, or a chorus of didgeridoos, an amplified recording of locusts chewing, the approach, passage and retreat of a thunderstorm, a computer-generated audio made from the pulsing light of a quasar, an orchestra of gamelans, a Georgian choir of women's voices, a muezzin calling the faithful to prayer, a cantor intoning the calendar's *Koren Siddur,* a quarter hour or more of Buddhist throat song from the steppes at Kyzyl Kum, a selection of Hopi, Hunkpapa or

Tlingit ceremonials. And from there on to something lapidary, usually, something he considered crystalline, a motet of Josquin, a madrigal of Gesualdo, something from the *Gymnopédies,* perhaps, a Lied of Schubert or melody from Mendelssohn's *Kinderszenen,* a quartet of Bartok, a Late Quartet of Beethoven, a Chopin nocturne, some Samba or Minnesang, something from Szymanowski or Britten's *Sea Interlude,* or Hertha Töpper's *Agnus Dei* from the *Mass in B minor.*

And most nights he'd end up in the company of Armstrong's Hot Five or Hot Seven, with Jack Teagarten or Roswell Rudd, Jimmy Hamilton, Russell Procope, Charlie Christian, The Art Ensemble of Chicago, Bud Powell, Steve Lacy or Cecil Taylor, Billie Holiday, Otis Redding, Leadbelly, the inevitable Francis Albert Sinatra. Sometimes he'd devote an entire show to a single performer, composer or lyricist: Hank Williams or Patsy Kline, Augustín Lara, Astor Piazzola, Umm Kulthum, perhaps, or Amália Rodrigues; or maybe Piaf, Aznavour, Brel; or Robert Johnson, Son House or Ma Rainey; the music of Billy Strayhorn, Thelonious Monk, Vernon Duke or Harold Arlen; the lyrics of Cole Porter, Johnny Mercer, Yip Harburg.

It didn't seem to matter. All he needed to do, it appeared, was to show up, and to nurse the little station's signal into the dawn. Because he was indeed in every sense the last of his kind, he'd often think, as he sat and listened, supplying sounds that no one seemed present to hear, noises issuing from this obscure little moribund enterprise, this perishing medium, sounds whose sources, human and inhuman, no one, perhaps, had ever heard or even heard of, much less thought about.

Each of his precisely sequenced programs, though, he knew, was something like a little universe, an elite little university of melody and meaning, ripe for the picking, available for free, should anyone happen onto his slender frequency at this unholy hour of the night.

And he remembered reading somewhere how radio signals never die. If this is to be believed, their languid vibrations can be imagined as something immaterial, insubstantial, sent wandering into the night, out over the sleepers and the insomniacs, over the rooftops of the dreaming city, over the cosmic hum of 2.725 degrees Kelvin, swept past all hearing, across the water, out past the reciprocating company of others, hurrying slowly, as if in keeping with that ancient prescription, a *festinare lente* that vanishes as it arrives, an unnoticed vibration carried along, as we all are carried, voice and flesh alike, past every point of no return, outward into the furiously expanding, quietly exploding dark.

Dawn Balloon at Anza-Borrego

In noiseless transit
through the quiet dawn
a Barn Owl crossed
beneath the drift
of our groaning basket
midnight's muffled thief
daybreak's sated raptor
patron of the desert's edge
rastering the scattered wood-
land's providential floor
on her glidepath home
from a night of stealth
and eager gourmandise
among the pulpy moths
unwary voles
and ill-starred moles.

For an instant
the downy aftershock
of that cameo appearance
held us breathless
in its predatory grasp
when jarringly the gas-
jet roared again
and a blinding ray
of daybreak cracked
the sky wide open
out behind the ridge
to annihilate the spell
encircle us with sight
imprisoning our ascent
into the panoramic grandeur
of that intrusive altitude

to blind us with
the distant prospects
of terrain uncloaked
by light disrobed
by the loud intrusions
of our awkward
lumbering conveyance
that bright balloon's
ephemeral dominion.

Yet in recollection's wake
dawn's silent owl
remains out there aloft
and glides untethered
uncontained across
some inner chamber
of the earthbound mind
the silent passage
of her soaring span
the momentary privilege
of our vanished
vantage place a world
away a world apart
forever fugal
endlessly recurrent
eternally fugitive
indelibly there.

Autumn Nocturne

Lhude sing Godamm!
—Ezra Pound

In stillness out past all the trees,
our lately flown Hesperides.

Anemones hang lank and black;
the season trumpets all we lack.

This wind's a mattress for the moon,
for every bleak, upholstered, ashen noon.

The lambent leaf, the bare pollarded tree,
the ragged shore, the tattered sea,

the croaking crow and laughing loon,
the turtle's cry, the mournful tune

of woeful dirges, plaint and evensong,
of lilting litany and psalm gone wrong.

Where similes can only gather dark,
no cunning metaphor can find the spark,

yet closer in, our daylight's tactile sun,
the clean perfume of clay upon the skin,

the acrid smoke of prunings, wormy pear,
the raptor's cry, a shrillness in the air,

dispels the pall of every nonspecific grief,
and bathes the night in balms of disbelief.

Lovesong, for Julie

The world occurred
          in the bluest interval
                    between wingbeats

                    in the incessant shorebreak

the persistent querying
of owls at dusk.

The world flashed out

                    between the notes
          of unfamiliar melody

                    in the sudden flurry
          of sudden leaves.

How lovely
          this sad weather

                    and each precisely
                    hungry raven

          in its turning sky

                    while this color-wheel
          of ice and linen

this ash-white light
        the slender climbing
                gull-grey towers

in the imperious distances
        forever turn and turn

                and it is always you
and only always me.

Envoi

So carry these scourings from the well of years,
from the unremembered, the immemorial,

from oblivion's boundless recollections,
from the endless aftershocks of sense.

Your mute desire is its speech,
each sonorous fantasy its consequence,

each utterance its recurrence, a residual of time,
that leaves its slender rhizomes
curling in delirium.

***

Your thoughts, these stands of shining poplars,
sway like Baptist choirs in the night,

like blue flame risen in the roaring world,
beneath the flashing sky, the hammering torrents,
the blue tin roof of sleep.

***

A stark idea glisters in the heaving soil, ignites
these tangled phosphors in the swarming tilth
to send the rushing senses into anxious rain
from what past threat? to what safe place?

in hot pursuit of who's lost voice?
in headlong flight from what forgotten pain?

VI.
Afterwords

L'à Venir

An apology for Caren

Yes, she said, smiling,
opening the little volume, *nice,*
but what's this all about?

About nothing at all, I suppose.
It's just what happens, not about it,
not at all a thing about.

Itself's what happens here,
the purling voice of what's not there,
a communiqué, as thinkers say

(for who knows where it's from?),
that's forever on its way, the approach
of what is always yet to come.

She Who Speaks

On a flyleaf among the Walmart bargain books

I am not the author of this book. Someone else must write it. Someday, perhaps. Or just as likely never. Perhaps it has almost been written. Maybe you, its reader, must complete it. Maybe, not being its author, I have no right to speak, no status here. Perhaps I'm not the authoritative voice, even in my denial, that you'd expect to be speaking, perhaps not even a character in this story. And yet here you are, face-to-face with what it is, a book among so many books. What it is or what it will be. Undeniably.

And there it lies, I imagine, quizzically, defiantly, perhaps a little uncomfortably, in your hands. It has a kind of reality, I suppose, a certain heft, a density of sorts, an odor of pulp and mystery. The edge of a page, of this dust jacket, handled wrong, can slice a finger . . . . but don't be misled by the bulk you're holding. That's just the measure of its peculiar insubstantiality: the scattered ink, the rustling pages, the thoughts, all the words it uses, their curious densities.

There's a winning innocence about you, I'm guessing, the way you fearlessly crack it open to a random page, let your eye drift down to a random spot, read a sentence or two, flip to another spot, forward to the Contents or the opening sentences, slap it shut, appreciate the cunning detail of its cover design at arm's length. You are fearless, that much is clear. Me, not so much. I've lived with it too long, perhaps, lived in it, beside it, beneath it.

The book is something like the sky, in my view. Or a thing like a sky. Like the blue monotony overhead, or like a lid, something fallen, something pressing. Its weight can isolate, release, repress. Depends on you, I suppose. Like some varieties of sky, it offers up its transitory sceneries. Its subject matter, its contents, appear like cloud, shape-shift, drift over the horizon, fade into indistinctness.

Its impersonality, its staggering indifference, is infinitely suggestive, endlessly referential. The scenes it presents to your imagination, like cloud, may suggest to you things familiar: a horse, a nose, a tree. But, like cloud, the recognizable images fade, dissolve, and reestablish, before you know it, their aura of stark impossibility, of remoteness and evasiveness, their annoying fragmentarity and bothersome urgency.

What is it about, this book? you probably wonder. Ahh. I was afraid you'd ask that. And I'm a little afraid to be obliged to answer. Because you may think I'm being insincere, abstruse, toying with you, or trying to be provocative. Let's see. To be about something is to not be the thing it is about, I guess, to stand apart from it. Here, I'd say, you have in hand a hopeless, paltry thing, something incapable of standing at an adequate distance from the things in it, from the world outside it, even from you perhaps, or from itself. I maintain it's something that isn't really even there, that only just approaches, comes near, from outside the realm of capability, detachment, effectiveness. Perhaps it's nothing but the substance of this very volatility it seems to describe, present, evoke in its way-too-many pages. Not something that follows an occurrence, as a philosopher has said, but that's itself an occurrence, the harbinger of its own irreducible futurity, always seemingly the voice of something somewhere up ahead, imminent but forever inactual.

And what's it *for,* then? you may reasonably ask, since you seem to be a reasonable person. What's it good for? To which I'm tempted to say, "for nothing," to say it's good for nothing at all. But this would sound far too arrogant, self-consciously avant-garde, insouciant, off-putting to the potential paying customer. Yet I'm obliged to admit that any value you might assign to it must belong to another dimension than the useful, to another system, another economy. It cannot help you fix a drain or illuminate the career of Metternich or John Wesley Powell, or be a calmer, kinder person.

It's you who must decide, I'm afraid, just what it might be good for. It's just one of those things, like many others perhaps, a canvas of Pollock, a Bud Powell solo, a sculpture of Anthony Caro or David Smith, the creak of floorboards in the night: something that leaves you to your own devices, absolutely alone, no help in sight. The only hope it offers you, I guess, perhaps your only real option, is that you come to regard it as a kind of door and not a space. A passage, not a place. An exit from the commonplace, a passage outward from the useful, the edifying, the familiar. But to where?

And here it's really up to you again, I reckon, to the slim possibility you will hear, somewhere in the curious noise it makes, in this strange assemblage of the words, a rustling sound that dwells already in your ear, the sound that living makes and, isolated as we creatures are, exotic as the common air, the distant rumor of this life we all must, one way or another, lead. What paltry reality it does have, you could say, is something metamorphic, transformative, a curious instance of the vague recurrences that return you somehow changed to exactly where you live.

The story here, dear reader, if story this be, is not mine in any personal sense, but your own. I, you must remember, don't quite exist. "You be the judge," as it says in Proust, "Did we get it right?" It's a tall order, I realize. And if you can spare that $5.99, it's really up to you. You are always free to set it back down on its stack, or anywhere at all on this crowded table. No questions asked. You, flesh and blood of all these words, citizen of the land of unfettered possibility, must decide.

About the Author

DB Jonas is the author of two previous poetry collections, *Tarantula Season and Other Poems* (Finishing Line Press, 2023) and *Flight Risk: Poems and Translations* (Kelsay Books, 2025). He lives in the Sangre de Cristo Mountains of northern New Mexico with his wife, their dogs, and their orchards.

Further examples of his work can be accessed at:
jonaspoetry.com

y

www.ingramcontent.com/pod-product-compliance
Lightning Source LLC
LaVergne TN
LVHW090519110826
845146LV00003B/918

* 9 7 9 8 9 0 1 4 6 7 1 2 1 *